A Textile Tra
guide to
PERU & BOLIVIA

Cynthia LeCount **Samaké**

Publisher: Linda Ligon
Associate Publisher/Editor: Karen Brock
Design: Ann W. Douden

Text ©2019 Cynthia LeCount Samaké
Photography, except as noted,
©2019 Cynthia LeCount Samaké

On the front cover: Mother, with daughter, knitting a *chullo* with pre-made bobbles, or *q'urpu*, Accha Alta, Peru.
On the title page: Clowns cavort in the bell tower of the Chinchero church at the festival of the Virgin of the Nativity.
On the opposite page: Wititi dancer in traditional dress from Chivay, Peru.

THRUMS
BOOKS

4420 Roaring Fork Court
Loveland, CO 80538

Printed in China by Asia Pacific
Library of Congress Control Number: 201895642

ACKNOWLEDGMENTS

Most importantly, my heartfelt thanks to the Andean villagers and the Bolivian Carnival performers who answered my questions and allowed me to photograph them. I also greatly appreciate the cooperative spirit of everyone who has helped compile this book; nobody said "no" to any of my requests!

Director Mario Amano and Curator Bruno Alva of the Amano Museo Textil Precolombino in Lima, and Susy Sano of the Museo Rafael Larco Herrera in Lima, all generously sent information and photos of fine museum specimens to include. Ana Mujica Baquerizo graciously identified a couple of mystery textiles for correct labeling. Veronica Samañez, Raul Rivera Velasquez, Diane Bellomy, Alice Hunt, Anthony Eitnier, Thomas Arnold, Sasha McInnes, Jack Wheeler, and several other people also kindly gave me permission to use images of textiles, textile artists, or festivals.

Claudia Avila and Gerardo Guzmán have accompanied me on many trips to the Andes and their good-natured support and expertise helped immeasurably; both of these friends have shared photos used here. The good team at Dreamstime also helped fill in the gaps where I didn't have the perfect photo on hand.

About 35 years ago, Nilda Callañaupa Alvarez introduced me to some wonderful knitters and weavers in the Cusco area; I am grateful for that connection and for her continuing friendship.

Editor Karen Brock patiently pored over photos and asked questions, guiding the book to greater usefulness. And always my daughter Alexis Nina Katrine was there telling Mom to "just chill." Huge thanks to all.

Contents

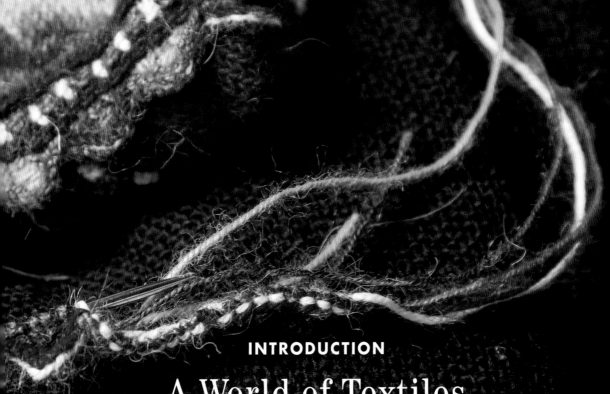

A World of Textiles

It's one thing to see spectacular textiles in museums but quite another
to watch a celebration of proud dancers decked out in handwoven
and handknitted festival gear or to visit a village where everyone
from toddlers to grandparents wears traditional clothing. This book
will help you find a wide selection of textiles in some of the best and
most exciting places of Peru and Bolivia. I explain how and where to
see and photograph festival celebrants wearing handmade, traditional
clothing, and where to buy it whenever possible. I also list the best
museums that contain collections of superb historical textiles that
inspire today's creations.

Colorful embroidered pillows from Ayacucho, Peru.

I have freely expanded the typical definition of textiles to include things such as the glitzy, embroidered satin costumes of Bolivia's Carnival (which also belong in the realm of fashion design) and the complex beaded and embroidered costumes of dancers in the Virgin of Carmen festival in Peru.

Most small shops and market stalls are full of items that are destined for tourists or travelers, mixed in with indigenous, village-made textiles. I consider visitors a positive force; without their economic input, thousands of textile artisans would cease to produce and sell, with grave consequences for their families and quality of life. For the tourist market, weavers and knitters create many innovative and carefully crafted wool or alpaca items that show up-to-date aesthetics and modern usage but which are based on traditional techniques. Tourist-destined textiles generally fall into categories of clothing or home décor, such as the exquisite embroidered pillows of Ayacucho, Peru, along with other items intended for tourist consumption.

I have featured traditional textiles as well as new, innovative pieces in an exciting mix, and everyone will be sure to find something of interest. Note that it is often easier to see indigenous textiles than to buy them, but finding the best "tourist textiles" is easy. I've listed many shopping destinations where you will find both types. For your enjoyment while traveling, I have also included some of my favorite hotels and restaurants. The hotels are all safe, comfortable, and reasonably priced, and in most cases, they are owned by people I have known for decades.

[Unless their comportment is offensive, I don't consider visitors/ tourists/travelers to be a negative element. In Peru, tourism comprises the third-largest industry after fishing and mining, and it employs 11 percent of the work force. If it weren't for tourists traveling to Peru and Bolivia, there would be far fewer textiles to love! And Peruvians who come to Machu Picchu from Lima are still called tourists; interestingly, the majority of tourists in Peru are from Chile. Travelers to Bolivia are mainly from Argentina and Peru. Americans and Europeans comprise a much smaller number of visitors.]

My Life of Travel and Textiles

Everyday travel in Bolivia.

I went to the Andean highlands for the first time in 1972, before Cusco, Machu Picchu, and Lake Titicaca had become hugely popular tourist destinations. I had graduated from college and was anxious to see the world. I traveled with local people and their sheep in the backs of trucks and ate tepid rice topped with a fried egg for dinner. Over the past 45 years, I have visited the Andes some forty times; much of this travel involved research in remote villages for my 1990 book, *Andean Folk Knitting: Traditions and Techniques from Peru and Bolivia*. Through the University Research Expeditions Program (UREP) based at the University of California, Davis, where I was teaching World Textiles, volunteers helped me during several field sessions to gather primary material while working toward my master's degree in festival costume of the Bolivian Carnival. Later in 1996, a yarn company in Vermont asked me to lead a knitting and textiles trip to Bolivia; every year since then I have accompanied groups of fiber enthusiasts to the Andes through my travel company, Behind the Scenes Adventures. Fortunately, in the last decade, travel has become much easier; roads and cuisine have improved, buses are more comfortable, and flights are less expensive.

Also, local entrepreneurs and international corporations have developed dozens of excellent places to eat and sleep. In short, Peru and Bolivia make fascinating, safe, and friendly destinations for travelers.

Concurrently, the lifestyle and economic situation of rural populations have improved over the last several decades, but to a lesser degree. Many villages still lack running water or schools, and farmers depend on unreliable rain for their crops. Despite outside influences—such as television, tourists, and readily available used or cheap imported clothing—indigenous people still proudly create and wear handmade clothing and textile accessories, especially for special occasions. Many villagers, typically the men, have adopted elements of western factory-made clothing, and you will see examples of this in the popular nylon parkas and baseball caps. But for festivals and weddings, both men and women in the countryside wear their best, traditional, handmade clothing. I encourage you to experience the excitement of this juxtaposition of tradition and modernity in today's Peru and Bolivia, on your own or with a group whose focus is textiles and fibers.

Finely knitted acrylic *chullo* from the Marcapata area of Peru.

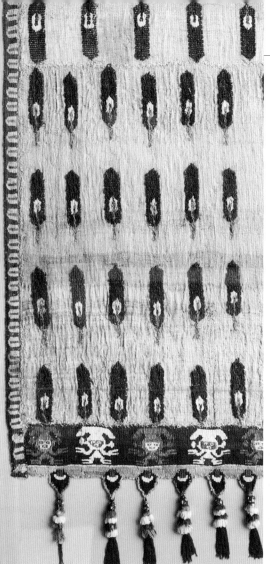

Chancay culture mantle from the north coast of Peru, CE 1000–1470.

Two Thousand Years of Textiles

Modern-day textile artisans in Peru and Bolivia continue the long tradition of textile excellence and expertise begun over 2,000 years ago by their ancestors. Ancient peoples from hundreds of different language and culture groups invented and perfected the use of every textile technique except knitting. The bulk of handwoven textiles was produced to envelop mummies; burial in the dry coastal sands preserved the cotton and alpaca fibers as well as the dyestuff hues used to pattern them. Fortunately, many stunning examples of these ancient textiles survived for us to appreciate. Coastal gravesites, or necropoli, such as those at Paracas-Nazca in the south and El Brujo in the north, divulged some of the most spectacular textile examples ever discovered. The 2,000-year-old Paracas mantle in the Brooklyn Museum's collection for example has ninety tiny, cross-looped figures with miniature clothes and accessories encircling its edges.

Spaniards arrived on the coast of South America in 1532 and claimed the land for the crown. Spanish rulers realized that governance in their vast new land would be easier if it were organized into territories or viceroyalties. In 1534, soon after the defeat of the Incas, the Viceroyalty of Peru was founded, allowing the Spaniards to delegate control of their enormous holdings and to dominate the inhabitants. (Another strategy of dominance was to build Catholic churches on top of indigenous temples, as Santo Domingo was built on top of *Korikancha*, the Inca sun temple in Cusco.)

The *encomienda* or forced labor system established throughout the territories placed indigenous people under the cruel authority of the Spaniards. They enslaved local weavers in sweatshops called *obrajes* and forced them to make religious vestments and tapestries with Iberian-Catholic motifs. At this point, over 500 years ago, many textile traditions and techniques such as gauze weave, intricate featherwork, crossed looping, and pieced tie-dye were lost. Now we can see examples of these ancient and complex techniques only in museums where intricate embroidery, weaving, looping, and knotting from ancient Peru and Bolivia thrill even the most jaded fiber fanatics.

Fragment of an embroidered feline on a Paracas textile from the collection of the Amano Museum.

Motifs from pre-Hispanic textiles, or from the weavers' ancestral storehouse or dreamworld of patterns, inspire many textile artisans. Fortunately, in Peru, artists such as Maximo Laura, and social entrepreneurs such as Nilda Callañaupa Alvarez are encouraging the creation and marketing of textiles with a contemporary appeal and are reviving ancient textile techniques in the process. As anthropologist Elayne Zorn explained, "Nowadays, weaving and other textile techniques are an outlet for artistic expression, a viable source of income, and a way to connect to pre-Conquest traditions."

The large, commercial enterprise, Incalpaca that produces wonderful baby alpaca yarn, has also revived pre-Hispanic motifs recently, in their Kuna line of scarves and sweaters designed with ancient textile patterns. Combined with lovely colors and soft fibers, the designs appeal to many who like very refined apparel. These products are made on industrial machines, but the stores have begun advertising with images of indigenous women at looms, along with fuzzy alpacas, for the "handmade" aura.

In Bolivia, knitters and weavers make textiles for their own use as well as those specifically for sale. A good example of this is the colorful wool tapestries woven by Tarabuco men. They blend pre-Hispanic images with imaginative depictions of animals and figures from their dreams to make delightful and popular pieces strictly for the tourist market.

Liz Rojas of Candelaria Tours explains a locally woven textile at the Tarabuco Sunday market.

Throughout Bolivia, people make traditional clothing and accessories for themselves, to be used for the period of time that the items are fashionable or presentable. Then the items may eventually (and rightfully) be offered for sale as authentic; the knitted caps of northern Potosí Department are a good example of this. Cap motifs change often and dramatically among the young men; the fashion-conscious sell last year's cap as soon as they knit a new and cooler version. Seeing and collecting contemporary costumes and indigenous textiles remain important objectives of many travelers to Peru and Bolivia.

Buying Textiles

Naturally, if you like textiles, you will want to buy pieces that are skillfully made or that have some redeeming design features. If you weave or knit, you are ahead of the game because you already know what good craftsmanship looks like. If you don't, or aren't used to looking at textiles, it can be hard to determine if a piece is handmade or commercially woven. For starters, if the cloth is in a bolt, it most likely came from a factory, but treadle-loomed woolen cloth is occasionally sold in bolts, too.

Selvedges can also help determine whether an item is handwoven. Metal teeth on industrial weaving machines grip the edges of the fabric during production; regular, tiny holes along the selvedges indicate that the cloth is factory-made. Most handmade pieces in the Andes have an edging, either woven into the sides of the cloth or added separately. The width of the piece is important too; handwoven textiles are not typically wider than about 12 to 22 inches per panel, due to the width of the looms used by handweavers. On a staked ground loom, weavers can make much wider pieces than with a backstrap loom, and a treadle-loom weaver in Peru or Bolivia can make pieces that are 3 to 4 feet wide depending on the loom. So on a wide poncho or carrying cloth, check to see if there are one or two decorative seams where the weaver has joined the panels. If a large cloth is one wide piece, like the colorful synthetic pieces sold everywhere, it is not handwoven. You might find a factory-woven piece of acrylic fabric that will make a stunning tablecloth that you can throw in the washer. Several stores in Cusco (probably in Lima and La Paz, too) offer factory-woven synthetic yardage in bolts in a huge variety of appealing color-stripe combinations, great for outdoor tablecloths or furniture, covers, pillows, and so forth.

Weaving on a backstrap loom in Pitumarca, Peru.

Fibers

We should start a discussion of fibers used in the Andes with some definitions. Alpaca is technically hair and sheep's coats are wool, and both can be called fiber. So if you hear in English, "alpaca wool," the term isn't technically correct. The Andean women add a funny bit to the terminology by saying "*lana de acrylica*" or acrylic wool, maybe hoping all you hear is "lana."

Bolts of industrially woven acrylic cloth in a Cusco shop on the road to the San Pedro Market.

You may not be able to distinguish pure alpaca fiber from man-made synthetic fibers, or from a blend of the two. Sometimes the distinction is glaringly obvious and other times the fiber type is really puzzling. Vendors may or may not know the difference and may or may not tell you the truth. The longer you spend chatting with a vendor and establishing a relationship, the more likely you will be to hear the real story. And you may not care about the fiber or provenance if you like the textile, but here are a few pointers to consider:

❖ There are a couple of ways to tell the difference between fibers beside the burn test that is difficult to do on a textile you don't yet own. When new, acrylic yarns either have a shine to them or they look very dull; when old, they fade, soften, and look much like cotton. So if possible, find a corner to pick at, or turn the piece over, or inside out in the case of a cap. Brilliant original colors in knitted items and a stiff hand with little drape to a woven item often indicate synthetic yarns. They are extruded as fibers from a man-made polymer mix that contains hues that can be shockingly bright: hot pink, Day-Glo chartreuse, orbit orange. This is what the villagers themselves want and what you will notice them wearing in their *awayos* (the Aymara word for carrying cloths, also called *lliqlla* in Quechua), ponchos, and caps—brilliant, intense, color.

❖ Natural fibers such as sheep's wool and alpaca can become *almost* as bright as acrylic yarn colors when dyed with chemical dyes, so color alone is not the best determinant. The tapestry weaving men of Tarabuco, Bolivia, dye the sheep's wool for their bright tapestries with chemical, aniline dyes, and weavers dye the wool for the thick woven blankets called *frazadas* with chemical dyes.

❖ Camelid hair from alpaca and llama has flatter, smoother scales than sheep's wool—think of a palm-like tree with very smooth bark. The dense, flat scales make alpaca fairly water-repellent and slightly

Acrylic yarn display in a Bolivian market. These yarns are often overspun by hand to eliminate most of the fuzz that would obscure a detailed woven or knitted motif.

Naturally dyed yarns dry in the courtyard of the weaving center in Chinchero, Peru.

A basket of yarns reflects the variety of colors achieved by using natural dyestuffs.

Colorful socks handknitted from commercially spun alpaca yarn, from the artisans' market in Huancayo, Peru.

dye-resistant, requiring a very hot dye bath for deeper tones. The more open scales help wool to absorb dye better resulting in more intense tones. I have dyed wool and alpaca in the same dye pot with natural dyes, and although the alpaca results in lovely colors, the wool ends up a more saturated color.

❖ Chemical dyes are available in most markets, stored in old cans and doled out by the spoonful, onto a little piece of paper. Vendors sell the powdered dyes, for example, at the corners of Illampu and Santa Cruz Streets in La Paz sitting behind white sample boards with vivid circles of various colors. Out in remote villages there is usually one person selling dye powders for his neighbors to color their natural fibers.

❖ Artisans knitting or weaving pieces designed to appeal to tourists often work with natural dyes to make subtle hues that some weavers call "gringo colors."

❖ To confuse the fiber puzzle, more factory-spun blends of acrylic and alpaca, in more colors, are available all the time. The Michell yarn company (see page 74) also sells cones of blended alpaca and acrylic yarns in dozens of colors at a much lower cost than pure alpaca. These less expensive, mixed fibers are strong for weaving. They also have the advantage of wearing and washing so well that knitters are using them more and more for tourist sweaters, scarves, and gloves. Artisans and vendors may insist that the yarn is alpaca, 100 percent. Some synthetic yarn companies now make yarns in more subtle colors also.

❖ It takes a microscope to definitively identify some fibers, and we don't need to get that carried away. If it appeals to you or feels good to wear, buy it and wash it carefully when it needs it.

I like the combinations of brilliantly colored acrylic yarns used by Andean artisans. And it's easy to understand why someone living in a mud-brick house on a tan-brown hill would prefer to add color to his or her life. Using sheep wool or alpaca hair entails shearing the beast by hand, washing the fleece, spinning it, then dyeing it over a smoky wood or llama dung fire before even beginning to work on the project. Dyeing at home with natural or aniline dyes involves huge pots and enough fuel for the fire. Naturally, many artisans prefer to buy the acrylic yarns that are available inexpensively in every market in every remote hamlet. Vendors offer little butterfly skeins and big balls of dazzling man-made colors, making an impressive array of colors possible in each project. You will notice this in particular with the clothes and accessories on dancers in Oruro during *Anata Andina* (pages 110–114).

An *awayo*, a carrying cloth, woven in Bolivia with overspun, acrylic yarn.

Knitters and weavers create finely knitted caps, intricately woven belts, and wildly patterned carrying cloths with these synthetic yarns. The makers know that the "gaudy" colors don't appeal to tourists, so they use their outstanding skills to make pieces for themselves. Working with acrylic yarn does involve some effort; most weavers and knitters overspin the fine acrylic yarn before

they work with it to eliminate the fuzz that might obscure an intricate design. If the patterns and colors of a textile make you happy, and you are not a fiber snob, a finely crafted acrylic piece will look just as beautiful on your wall as an alpaca piece.

Where You Will Find Textiles to Buy

You'll probably discover two settings in which to purchase your textiles. The first is in a shop or market where the textile is removed from its maker and sold by a middleman. Vendors in some places offer great selections of excellent textiles from many parts of the Andes. But most of them buy from traveling textile dealers, and thus they may not know the fiber content, use, or provenance of a piece. (Bolivian textiles have made their way to Cusco in the past few years, and the vendors always say they are Peruvian.) On the other hand, some vendors are very knowledgeable and can give you good information about the textiles they sell.

The other kind of textile you might want to purchase is new, made recently, and sold directly by the person who created it—or by an agent acting in their best interest, such as a nonprofit organization. If you visit a village and textiles are offered for sale, you can meet the artisan, see the processes, and feel a connection with the person, the place, and the piece once you get home. To help weavers and knitters continue to make a living when they produce only for the tourist market—for example, making placemats or alpaca *chullos* (knitted hats) that they don't typically use—buy at a recognized fair-trade store whenever possible.

The Center for Traditional Textiles in Cusco (CTTC) is one such fair-trade place where the artisans get a fair price for their superb work, and they take pride in continuing their tradition of handmade textiles. All pieces for sale at CTTC have been washed and go through a rigorous quality check to ensure that they are exceptional textiles. Each item has a name tag and you can imagine the money for your purchase going to help that specific person have a better life. Yes, you might find woven pieces of dubious fiber quality at a lower price elsewhere, but it feels good to value your gorgeous CTTC textile, knowing you are helping a family to feed and educate the children. There are a couple of other smaller endeavors that market village-made textiles (see pages 56–57).

[Over a decade ago, weavers and/or vendors decided to cater to Westerners' taste for more "earthy" colors with an overdyeing technique also used on handwoven textiles in Thailand and Laos. Somebody correctly assumed that travelers might prefer softer greens, mellow whites, and toned-down pinks, so they started dipping handwoven but "too colorful" woolen blankets (and an occasional awayo) in an orange dyebath. The idea caught on and resulted in a plethora of orange overdyed textiles. The original motifs and patterns are still visible, and the stripes show blended hues: orange on brilliant pink equals a softer peachy color, for example. You may see stacks of orangish blankets in some shops; there's nothing wrong with them if you like the colors; just know what you are getting.]

Above: Weavers from Pitumarca, Peru, warp a loom together.
The weaver will work in the discontinuous warp technique to
weave the *chakana*, or cross design.
Below: A handknitted chullo from Bolivia shows an incomplete
boat motif, which may indicate an inexperienced knitter.

Judging the Quality of a Textile

No matter where you buy a textile, it's good to
know how to judge the quality. For a woven piece,
be sure it lies fairly flat and has straight edges
with no frayed or snagged places, and no holes.
The designs should be crisp and clear even if
woven in subtle colors. Red dyes are especially
prone to run or bleed, causing the white areas of a
textile to turn pink. This can look fine unless the
fugitive dye makes unsightly blotches and spots.
A piece with an added handwoven edging has
taken twice as long to complete as a weaving with
simple selvedges, and so it is worth more. After
that, it's pretty much up to your personal taste. Do
you like muted colors and vague motifs, or do you
want something bolder?

Knitted caps considered for purchase should be
smooth and not buckled or lumpy; they should be
neatly knitted with even decreases all the way to
the top. Turn a cap inside out to see if brilliant
colors indicate that it's made of acrylic. See if the
knitter twisted or wrapped colors on every stitch
on the inside or left long, sloppy floats between
color changes. Partial designs in some rows of a
chullo mean that the knitter was inexperienced
and didn't plan well; these incomplete motifs can
be disconcerting or charming, like the half-cat
that smiles out of one chullo I have. Occasionally
you'll find one with a smaller but complete motif
to fill in the extra space when a larger motif won't
fit. Note that some caps now for sale in Cusco
were made in Bolivia. Still, you might find and buy
a great piece, and if the vendor doesn't know what
area it is from (or won't admit it is not Peruvian),
you still have a treasure. (If you want to identify it,
you can check the color plates in my *Andean Folk
Knitting* book to see if a similar chullo is there.)

If a knitted or woven textile is ripped or otherwise
shows its wear and you still want to buy it, perhaps

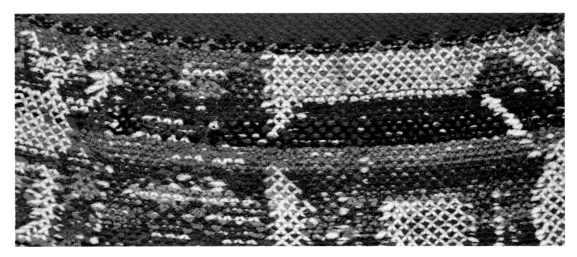

Inside of a chullo from Bolivia, showing how the knitter twisted every stitch of three colors to completely eliminate floats. This method naturally makes a thick and somewhat rigid cap.

you or someone else can repair it. You can ask the vendor if she knows someone who could repair it for you for a small price. Don't worry about a bit of grunge; I machine-wash synthetic caps with laundry detergent in a net lingerie bag and they come out beautifully. Even a larger synthetic piece, such as an awayo, can be washed in the machine on the gentle cycle. Don't use a dryer, but shape pieces with your hands and let them air-dry. You can also gently handwash woolen or alpaca pieces with lukewarm water and Ivory Snow or Flakes.

Tourist-destined "ancient" figure, showing bits of real pre-Hispanic cloth: fine tapestry shard for a headband and interlocking bird patterned fragment for the blouse. Skirt is native brown cotton, and a tiny flamingo feather remains stitched on at the bottom. Buying these figures encourages looters to continue sifting through archaeological sites.

Before you make a large textile purchase, look around town and talk to a few friendly vendors to see what else is available at what price. Then go back and bargain, and buy it if you still love it.

The Ancient and the Illegal

There is a possibility that you may ask about a textile in a market or shop and be told it is "*muy ancient, pre-Hispanico*." Very, very few antique pieces exist in shops today, and most of them are not ancient at all. You shouldn't buy them anyway, even if real, because it's illegal to take them home. Know that no textile deemed pre-Hispanic can be made of sheep's wool because sheep came to South America with the Spanish sailors.

Doll-like figures made with bits of cloth and sticks for arms are for sale in some markets; they were made yesterday, but their clothing is stitched together from tidbits of truly ancient fabric from coastal gravesites. They are copies of actual figures found in graves, which always have a tapestry-woven face and not the embroidered features of these fakes. Better not to buy them because that encourages looters to search for more fabric shards. (It is also illegal to take home the impaled insects and butterflies pinned in glass frames that are available at the market at Machu Picchu, among other places.)

My Personal Rules for Buying Indigenous Textiles

My first rule is never to buy anything that a villager is wearing on his or her body, even if they offer it to you when you admire it. You may or may not agree with this, but using the example of the chullos that the young men knit, I fear that if we buy a man's hat off his head (he may not have planned to sell it, or may not be ready to part with it, but he wants the money we are offering), he may never find the time to make another, and he'll decide to wear a trucker hat. Then we will be guilty of playing a small part in the westernization of indigenous people. Of course, selling his cap is a choice he is free to make, and both change and innovation will happen inevitably. This can be argued back and forth, but that is my rule for textile purchases.

My second rule is that I don't bargain if I am buying directly from the maker. The weaver or knitter knows how much time and materials went into the piece for sale; it's more than we could ever imagine. In my head, I often compare prices to the cost of a latte at home. For example, the asking price for handknitted gloves that a woman spent two days making is less than what I would pay for a coffee. How could I ask her if she would accept three dollars instead of four?

If the asking price seems high, know that the maker is still getting a pittance in exchange for his or her time. Rural people often struggle to feed their families or buy school supplies, and a few dollars can help immeasurably, so I usually err on the side of generosity. Occasionally, I meet someone on a trip who intends to buy items directly from artisans for resale. This suggested no-bargaining policy goes for those entrepreneurs, too; the artisans still do the same work, regardless of whether someone is buying one item or twenty. Prices are usually quite

Man wearing a chullo handknitted with motifs and structure typical of Chinchero, Peru.

A girl from Accha Alta, Peru, wearing the traditional dress of her community.

reasonable in any case, and I urge you to buy directly from the artisans whenever possible. On the other hand, if I am in a shop owned by a middleman (and most shops are), I do bargain, offering 20 to 25 percent less than the asking price, depending on the item.

I agree with travel writer Jeff Greenwald who says, "Bargain fairly, and with respect for the seller. Again, remember the economic realities of where you are. The final transaction should leave both buyer and seller satisfied and pleased. Haggling for a taxi or carpet is part of many cultures; but it's not a bargain if either person feels exploited, diminished, or ripped-off."

Taking Photos

It's much more polite to make some connection with a person before you stick your camera or phone in his or her face. A suggestion for street photography is to find a place to sit or stand and let the people pass by, entering and leaving your space. Photographing even in a market can be tricky because the vendor may or may not consider her tomatoes as personal, private property. Some will smile and pose with their goods and others will firmly indicate that no photos of vegetables or anything else will be allowed. Their attitude may depend on their previous interactions with people taking photographs.

If someone says "No," then smile, respect his or her wishes, and carry on with your day.

The man I met on the streets of Cusco who let me photograph his beautiful beaded hat ties, which are typical of Huilloc, near Cusco, Peru.

I don't pay people to take their photos, although attitudes about this differ. See what you think about the women hanging around the Cusco plaza asking for photos and money. They are dressed up in indigenous clothing, often have a couple of dolled-up kids with them, and are usually leading a bewildered baby alpaca on a leash.

Happily, festival participants love the limelight. They are on display and ready to show off, or they wouldn't be there. People in these venues almost universally accept being photographed (many will stop and pose) as long as you don't get in the way, interrupt the choreography, or crash into a musician who can't see over his sousaphone. Often a good place to photograph is at the beginning or end of the parade route when dancers are more relaxed. If there is no set procession, just hang out at the edges of the festivities, occasionally moving around to take a shot, then quickly getting out of the way.

But if the celebrants seem very inebriated, keep on walking because they might become unpredictable and truculent. Beer is an important part of every festival—for the thirsty dancers and as an offering to *Pachamama*, the Earth Mother. Naturally, you have a better chance of meeting sober dancers early in the day, and of course everyone does not drink to excess. Wait to be invited to attend Carnival group after-parties or family celebrations; don't walk in just because it looks like a convivial scene. Use caution about taking photos of Catholic or indigenous religious ceremonies anywhere; you may not be welcomed, especially at the latter.

If you are able to greet people and explain why you are interested in taking a picture (and here language helps), then you have a better chance at a good photograph. If you don't speak Spanish, you can get creative with gesticulation and friendly smiles. In Cusco recently, a friend and I saw two men in typical red ponchos and chullos walking across the street from us. I took a few shots they didn't notice from far across the street, and then I realized that I needed a better photo of them. So I dashed across and explained that I study knitted caps and would love a photo to use in my book about chullos. The man with particularly beautiful beaded hat ties agreed and stood there patiently while we took his photo. I showed him the image, thanked him, shook hands, and we all went on our way. I was so happy with his generosity that I totally forgot to get his name, which I like to include with portraits.

Another person might have thought I was a crazed foreigner and denied me the photo, but this man responded to my friendly, candid approach. I wish Polaroid cameras would come back in the original format because instant prints made wonderful presents for people that I photographed. Today, if I know the villagers or family, I get photo prints made at home and give them back on my next visit.

A Word about Language

People of Peru and Bolivia speak Spanish, Quechua, Aymara, and several dozen indigenous languages. In larger urban centers, most people will speak Spanish, but in more rural locations, residents may not. Quechua and Aymara are the most commonly spoken languages after Spanish. However, there is no clear division as to where each language is spoken. In Lake Titicaca, for example, those living on the Uros Islands speak Aymara, and on neighboring Taquile Island, Quechua is spoken. I use Quechua, Aymara, and Spanish terms somewhat interchangeably. The glossary (see page 141) defines foreign terms used throughout the book, noting the language. The terms I use are based on what I commonly hear in the locations I frequent in both countries.

Revelers at Carnival in La Paz, Bolivia, perform the Chutas dance.

Gifts and Giving

People who travel often want to give away things—candy and ballpoint pens are common culprits. However, just handing out goodies in the street to kids or to people you have no previous contact with encourages and perpetuates begging. Children who receive something simply because they ask for it learn a negative lesson fast and become very annoying to the next tourist who happens along. Plus, it's difficult to know how to give fairly; my suggestion is not to give anything directly to kids but instead to their parents or teachers. They know how to best distribute the items fairly, to avoid creating jealousy among siblings and envy in the community.

A toddler from the Peruvian highlands carried on her mother's back in the traditional handwoven *lliqlla*

But travelers who come to the Andes often want to bring something to offer to the people who take the time to share their homes or meals or weaving and knitting techniques. Westerners love to be generous; Americans are among the most generous people in the world, and it makes everyone feel good to offer something to someone who truly needs and/or appreciates it. So the answer here is yes, do give things that you know are needed, to adult villagers or to parents and teachers in charge of children. Try to respect local culture; for example, don't give baseball caps to village kids who traditionally wear handknitted caps.

If you are visiting villages, any of the following will be welcomed (most anywhere in the world): sewing supplies, good scissors, needles, heavy buttonhole thread, used or new knitting needles, hair barrettes; hotel mini-size soaps, shampoos and lotions; composition books, crayons, and pads of paper. Perhaps you have access to new or gently used generic reading glasses (not odd Rx glasses) or school/office supplies, or your dentist will give you dozens of sample toothbrushes or little tubes of toothpaste.

If you stay at Cusco's Hotel Marqueses (or some others around town who also have programs to help street kids, usually boys), you can bring gently-used clothes or shoes—these are city boys, not villagers—perhaps your own children's or grandchildren's hand-me-downs. These will be given out according to need and size, by Dr. Quintana (see page 59).

Check out Jeff Greenwald's "13 Tips for the Accidental Ambassador." He has excellent and succinct suggestions about how to be a sensitive traveler and how to make travel more rewarding for yourself and more gratifying for the people you encounter.

www.ethicaltraveler.org

Traveling Alone

Don't hesitate to travel alone! I went to Peru and Bolivia many times by myself when doing field research for my knitting book and had no problems. At first my parents and husband worried, but instead of danger, I discovered warm-hearted, generous, and solicitous people. You'll meet more people and you'll learn more of the local language than if you were distracted by a travel partner continually speaking your language. Because you are alone, families will befriend you, people will feel protective (and very sorry for you!) and will take extra care to help you. In a big city I remember needing to visit an ATM after dark and the hotel desk clerk insisted the elevator guy go with me, since I was alone and it was late.

If you are working on a knitting project, so much the better; this becomes a great icebreaker on a park bench or a long train ride. Try winding yarn from a skein; women all over the world can't resist holding out their hands to stretch the yarn, as you wind. Pull out your knitting, they will be fascinated by the yarn, especially if it's the magic computer-printed self-patterning sock yarn. If you don't knit, bring some yarn and needles and ask for advice; everyone knows the basics and you'll make friends while learning something new. In tiny villages where I landed while searching for traditional knitting, people opened up spare rooms with skinny beds for me and shared their quinoa soup. (This is a good time to bring out the little hotel soaps and shampoo presents you have brought.) Use common sense, dress in simple clothes like jeans and sweaters, don't flaunt your expensive and tempting things, and you'll have a completely different experience by traveling alone.

Be Here Now

I feel that I have a more meaningful adventure if I can remember to "be here now." I've seen people arrive at a hotel and demand the Wi-Fi code while the clerk is trying to check in the group. They scroll down phones to see the latest sports scores or grim political news, not even noticing the magnificent seventeenth-century walls of the heritage hotel. Or they spend an entire van ride over stunning scenery engrossed in a contest conversation about the last trip to Bhutan or Madagascar and miss the view. Unless there is an ongoing medical issue at home, you really don't need daily updates. Try to disconnect from home while you are traveling. Shut off your phone and don't use the hotel TV; you'll be more relaxed and you'll remember and appreciate your journey and its destination.

A knitter from Sallac, Peru, marvels at Nancy Thomas's latest hat project, while she admires his fine work. Sharing projects as you travel is always a great icebreaker and learning adventure for all.

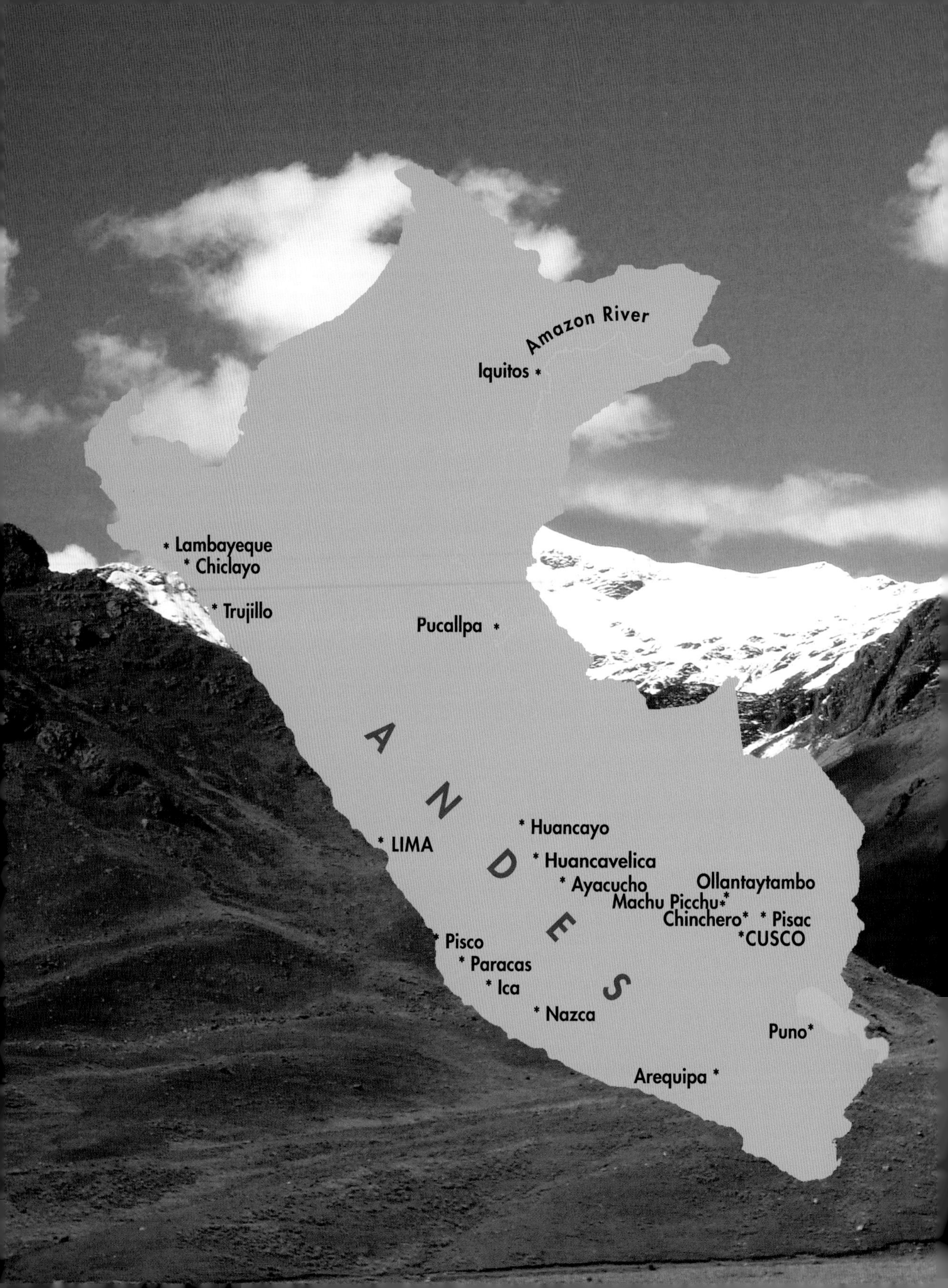

Amazon River

Iquitos *

* Lambayeque
* Chiclayo

* Trujillo

Pucallpa *

A N D E S

* Huancayo

* LIMA

* Huancavelica
* Ayacucho

Ollantaytambo
Machu Picchu*
Chinchero* * Pisac
*CUSCO

Pisco
* Paracas
* Ica

* Nazca

Puno*

Arequipa *

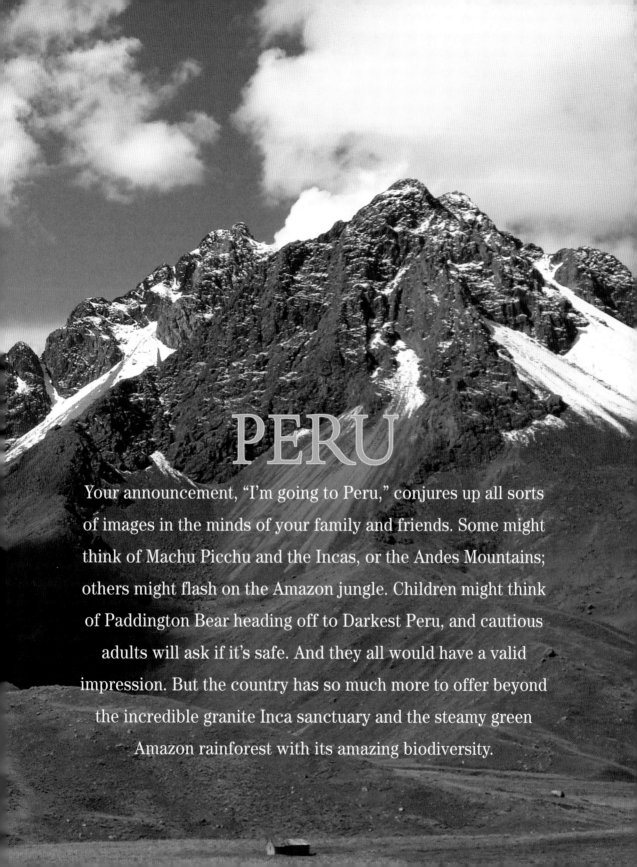

PERU

Your announcement, "I'm going to Peru," conjures up all sorts
of images in the minds of your family and friends. Some might
think of Machu Picchu and the Incas, or the Andes Mountains;
others might flash on the Amazon jungle. Children might think
of Paddington Bear heading off to Darkest Peru, and cautious
adults will ask if it's safe. And they all would have a valid
impression. But the country has so much more to offer beyond
the incredible granite Inca sanctuary and the steamy green
Amazon rainforest with its amazing biodiversity.

Peru is an economically stable and almost-always safe land of stunning vistas and stark contrasts. Andean highlanders who speak Quechua or Aymara subsist in mud brick houses, growing quinoa and weaving their own traditional clothing. Townspeople live alongside ornate colonial churches in UNESCO Heritage cities with cobblestone streets and Spanish-style plazas with flowers and fountains. And in coastal Lima, Peruvian families might live on the 32nd floor in sleek, ocean-view apartment towers, speak English without an accent, and send their teens to school in the United States.

On my most recent trip, we wound through the Andes for ten hours on rutted gravel roads, passing a couple of five-house hamlets bordered with rock walls. We overlooked alpine lakes and traversed valleys so high that the only sign of life was prickly ichu grass and grazing llamas. Eventually we arrived beachside, in the capital city of Lima with skyscrapers and commuter traffic. All of a sudden the country's population figure of thirty-two million people seemed possible.

Getting there

When you go to Peru, your flight will land in Lima. Don't be daunted by this huge metropolis. You will see that Peru's capital city has a balmy climate, friendly people, flowery parks, surfer-thrill beaches, world-class museums, and renowned restaurants. The following information will make your visit easy and pleasurable.

Checking in at your home airport

When you check in for your Lima flight, keep the little baggage claim sticker in a safe place because

they might ask for it in Lima when you exit the airport, to be sure you have your own luggage. I stick it into the back of my passport for safekeeping.

Planning your trip

Many airlines serve Lima's Jorge Chávez International Airport. Avianca, Copa, and LATAM are all good choices if they depart from your home city, and the layovers aren't too long. Sometimes many flights arrive all at the same time, and the immigration line snakes out into the hallway.

There are no evening flights to Cusco, so if that is your next destination, you'll need to spend the night in Lima. The Wyndham Costa del Sol in Lima is a convenient and pricey hotel at the airport. Or you can go to Magdalena del Mar or Miraflores to a safe and recommended hotel and enjoy Lima's great museums and restaurants before heading to other destinations. The

Stately colonial homes grace the Magdalena del Mar neighborhood in Lima.
Above: Eking out a living in rocky terrain at 11,000 feet.

route from the airport to Miraflores or downtown Lima (and back) takes about 45 minutes without traffic. At rush hour, the trip can take up to 2 hours.

Arriving in Lima

The plaza in front of the Governor's Palace in Lima.

Peru has recently changed immigration policies, and the authorities have made it much easier for tourists to visit. There are no longer visa requirements for most travelers and you can stay up to 6 months at a time. Citizens of the United States, Canada, Mexico, all South American countries, all countries within the European Union, the United Kingdom, Switzerland, the Asian countries of Japan, Laos, Malaysia, Philippines, Singapore, and Thailand plus Australia and New Zealand do not need a visa to enter Peru. Regulations change occasionally so check to be sure this information is current or if your country is not listed.

When you get off the plane, follow the crowd to Passport/Immigration. They'll ask why you are visiting and how long you will stay—"Tourism" or "Machu Picchu" for two weeks plus are good answers. They'll stamp your passport with a visa/entry stamp for anywhere from 30 to 90 days (free, no photos or money required). If you plan on a longer stay in Peru, tell them you need a 6-month stamp. Continue through the duty-free shop, out to baggage claim/pick-up. Follow the others from the flight. Security or airport workers will guide you along the route if you're confused; it is quite straightforward, and the airport is small.

Pick up bags at the baggage claim carousel for your flight. Bags can take quite a while to arrive, so if you have time, walk a bit to the left to a cambio/change kiosk and get some Peruvian money, soles; $40 is a good amount to start with. Note that in Peru, money conversion is easy: hand them your currency and they calculate and hand you soles, no passport or paperwork needed. The airport will not have the best exchange rates. See page 30 for more about money.

Taxis can be paid and tipped in dollars so don't worry if you can't get some soles at the airport. Note: You do not need to get soles from your bank at home before you arrive in Peru, and besides, the exchange rate will be very low there.

Once you have your bags, head left to the line for exiting. There you might have to put bags in the scanning machine, but if you look innocuous, they will most likely just wave you on. Occasionally, they want to look through bag contents—no problem unless you are carrying illegal drugs, pornography, or firearms. They don't seem at all interested in the normal tourist's supply of pills in any sort of container, or cameras or other typical travelers' items.

An artisan weaving a *golon*, the traditional edging for a woman's skirt.

Take a minute to get organized, and put your passport back in your secret pouch before you exit the customs area.

Transportation into Town
TAXI GREEN

Don't go beyond the taxi counters yet; walk all the way left to the prominent Taxi Green counter, or look for it if they have moved it elsewhere; ignore the others. Show the dispatching clerk at the desk your hotel name and address, and he or she will have you pay according to your destination, in dollars or soles. Miraflores rides and most other destinations in Lima are around $20 or 60 soles. The dispatcher will show you to your specific, private driver for that ride; it will be all logged in and organized. The drivers for Taxi Green are trustworthy and their late-model cars are spotless. You don't pay the driver anything when you arrive at your destination; he won't argue or hassle you (because you paid at the authorized Taxi Green kiosk), and you are totally safe. I always give the driver a $5 tip if he is friendly and helpful. One Taxi Green driver surprised me by stopping to buy a bottle of water when I was having a coughing fit!

www.taxigreen.com.pe
counterinternacional@taxigreen.com.pe
TEL: +51 1 5001691

LIMA AIRPORT EXPRESS

There is a new inexpensive Lima Airport Express bus service, popular for the price and the Wi-Fi on board, but it does not drop you at your hotel. It has seven drop-off points in Miraflores; this is fine for travelers with just a backpack, but you might have to walk a long way to find your hotel. Cost to and from the airport is $8.

www.airportexpresslima.com

UBER

Uber is available in Lima, but it's not terribly reliable, and some of the cars are junky.

Favorite Restaurant at Lima Airport

TANTA by Gaston Acurio

Go up the escalator at the far right end of the small airport. It has very friendly waiters, excellent food, snacks, sandwiches, full meals, and drinks. Prices are reasonable and dress is very casual. It is located across from the chair massage, which is also recommended.

Money in Peru

You can bring cash in bills from your home country or just use an ATM card; I do both. Be sure it's a debit card that has no foreign transaction fees because they can mount up. A reminder: when you bring cash, be sure the bills are clean and have no tiny tears, rips, ink marks, or scrawled love notes, or they will not be accepted. Large bills sometimes get a better exchange rate than small bills. Also, US$100 bills with a CB serial number will not be accepted because a long time ago, they were counterfeited. Check before you go.

The currency of Peru is the *sol* (sun); the plural is *soles*. You can print out a little soles travel conversion chart at www.oanda.com or use a phone app to convert. Banknotes come in denominations of 10, 20, 50, 100, and 200. One sol (S/.1) is divided into 100 céntimos, and coins are available in various small denominations; 50 céntimos is worth about 16 to 17 cents in the quite stable Peruvian currency world. Occasionally, you'll get change including a little coin that is 5 or 10 céntimos; save it to add to the coins for beggars or take them home to coin-collecting kids so they can learn some geography. There are also coins of 1, 2, and 5 soles that have designs of the Nazca hummingbird on them.

You can change bills in three types of places: a bank, an exchange kiosk, which is a little store called a *casa de cambio*, or on the street. Banks have long lines and are not a good option. You'll get a better rate in Lima with a street money changer, totally legal, but you should change in the right places, basically in Miraflores along Jose Larco Avenue and all around Kennedy Park. I change amounts of $100 or less with any of the people who have the official money-changer (*cambista*) maroon vests on. These novel new vests indicate that the cambista has registered with Miraflores officials. The vest also has a QR scan code so authorities can check to be sure the changer is legally registered and know if he or she is working in the right location. Better yet, the cambistas have an electronic emergency button to press to alert Miraflores central security center and the two local police stations if they are being threatened. The system is very impressive.

I have never had a problem with a money changer shortchanging me or giving me fake bills; they usually stamp their initials or code on each bill, and theoretically, you can return to them if you have a fake bill. I am careful to put the money away before I leave the cambista's presence and they help you to not flash the money around. If you are not in Miraflores or you need a lot of cash, find an ATM or a *casa de cambio*. ATMs (*cajero automático*) usually give good exchange rates. Some of the better hotels will change money if you are a guest. Outside of Lima, use the casas de cambios. Traveler's checks are useless, as they involve interminable waits at banks where they don't know what to do with them.

Your smartphone will probably work fine in Peru; be sure to keep it on airplane mode unless you are using it, so you don't run up hugely expensive roaming charges. Call your provider to get an international plan for the least expensive calling and texting. International calls are now between 35 cents and a dollar a minute on most plans. Texting works better and is less expensive. Most hotels in Peru now have free wireless internet, although it will be slower than you are used to at home. Some hotels have a computer set up for guests to use. You can also connect to Wi-Fi with a tablet or phone.

A fuzzy white alpaca communicates with her cousin the llama, asking, "How could they ever confuse me with you?"

Communicating

The best way to stay in touch with family and friends at home is through texting, Facebook messenger, FaceTime, or your personal email, which can be checked daily, even at Machu Picchu. Most areas in Peru have great internet connections, but reception is not always the best in the mountains or more remote areas.

WHATSAPP is a free app that you may want to download on your phone; you can call or text anyone else who has it for free any time you have Wi-Fi or a data signal available.

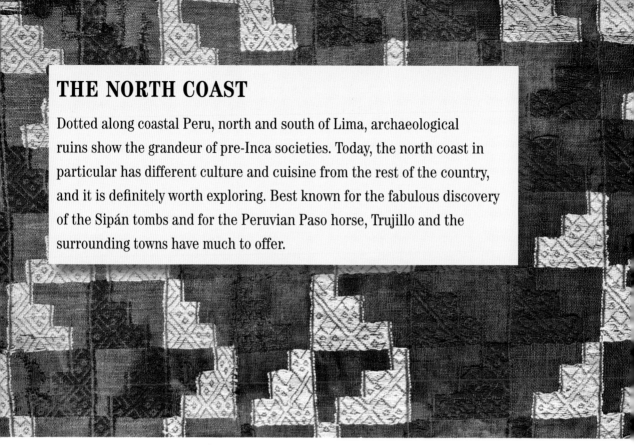

THE NORTH COAST

Dotted along coastal Peru, north and south of Lima, archaeological ruins show the grandeur of pre-Inca societies. Today, the north coast in particular has different culture and cuisine from the rest of the country, and it is definitely worth exploring. Best known for the fabulous discovery of the Sipán tombs and for the Peruvian Paso horse, Trujillo and the surrounding towns have much to offer.

Chancay culture fragment (CE 1000–1470). Native brown cotton with patterning in natural white and dyed red cotton thread. This is the back view of the piece, showing weaving floats and the small diamond-shaped faces of serpents or felines.

Getting there

The easiest way is the inexpensive 1-hour flight from Lima; the cheapest way is by bus. I usually fly from Lima to Trujillo and back to Lima from Chiclayo, which eliminates the need to backtrack. You can do the same route on the excellent Cruz del Sur bus line for about $35 and 9 to 10 hours each way.

Getting around the North Coast – Trujillo, Chiclayo, Lambayeque

Trusted driver and longtime friend **Marco Ramos** will follow your personal itinerary with private transportation for one person or a whole group. He has very good vehicles, including a midsize bus that holds up to twenty-four people. Marco drives carefully and lives in Trujillo, so he knows his way around to archaeological sites, museums, and restaurants in the whole northern area. Each archaeological site has guides to hire on the spot when you arrive; Marco can help you with that, too. He'll pick you up at the Trujillo airport, you can take a few days to see the sites, and then he will return you to the Chiclayo airport (or vice versa) in time for your flight back to Lima; this avoids backtracking. These "open-leg" flights coming into Trujillo and departing from Chiclayo are about the same price as a round trip. Marco is quick to respond to Facebook messaging or cell calls.

MARCO RAMOS
CELL/WHATSAPP: +51 937468994
marcoramos0311@gmail.com
Facebook: Marco Antonio Ramos Alva

Archaeological Site Museums with Pre-Columbian Textiles

EL BRUJO ARCHAEOLOGICAL COMPLEX/
Complejo Arqueológico El Brujo

In 1990, archaeologists began excavating at the Moche culture's large coastal site called El Brujo and found numerous textile-wrapped mummy bundles. In 2006, one special bundle held a discovery that surprised and thrilled the team: a 1,600-year-old female with tattooed skin. Archaeologists presume the "Señora de Cao" was a warrior because of her symbolic tattoos and the weapons and accoutrements found with her. You can visit the tombs where the mummies were found, with painted symbols still on the walls. The **Museo Señora de Cao**, which opened in 2009, is a superb modern museum that has contextual displays, the female warrior's intact body, and hundreds of grave objects, including some textiles. It is an excellent cultural experience and I highly recommend it. Over 3,000 textile pieces have been discovered at the site.

The whole archaeological complex at El Brujo is fascinating to explore, consisting of the sacred burial sites or huacas of *Huaca Cao Viejo*, *Huaca Prieta*, and *Huaca Cortada*. Archaeological excavations and research at El Brujo are ongoing.

www.elbrujo.pe/en/
TEL: +51 939326240
HOURS: Daily, 9 a.m.–5 p.m., except Christmas and New Year's
MUSEUM GENERAL ADMISSION: 10 soles; university students and seniors: 5 soles; school children: 1 sol
GETTING THERE: Lambayeque and nearby Chiclayo are 132 miles (212 km) from Trujillo north along the coast, about a 4-hour drive.

> **FUN FACT:**
> The world's oldest indigo-dyed textile (6,200 years old) was found at Huata Prieta, part of the El Brujo archaeological complex.

ROYAL TOMBS of SIPÁN MUSEUM/The Museo Tumbas Reales de Sipán

In 1987, some of the most extraordinary tombs in the world were found in *Huaca Rajada* (Sipán), a Moche archaeological site on the north coast, which predates the Inca by some 1,000 years. While a whole complex of unplundered burials has now been excavated, the most famous belongs to the "Lord of Sipán," a Moche warrior priest who was buried with an incredible wealth of artifacts.

The modern, three-story Royal Tombs of Sipán Museum (*Museo Tumbas Reales de Sipán*), shown above, opened in 2002 in the north coast town of Lambayeque to hold the treasure from the Sipán tomb excavations. Displays are stunning; life-sized figures complete with sumptuous textiles/clothing and accessories make the culture come to life. Reconstructed excavation pits show the professionals' digging processes and techniques. This is an excellent experience, highly recommended.

ADDRESS: Juan Pablo Vizcardo y Guzman 895, Lambayeque
www.museotumbasreales.com
TEL: +51 74 283977 or +51 74 283978
HOURS: Tuesday–Sunday, 9 a.m.–5 p.m.; closed Monday
ADMISSION: Adults: 10 soles; students: 4 soles
GUIDED TOUR available for 20 soles
GETTING THERE: Lambayeque and nearby Chiclayo are 132 miles (212 km) from Trujillo north along the coast, about a 4-hour drive.

Shopping

Monsefú Handicraft Market (*Mercado Artesanal de Monsefú*) is located in the small town of the same name, about 10 miles (16 km) south of Chiclayo. It's a group of twenty or so kiosks, known for their straw baskets, finely woven hats, and other handmade items. You can also wander around the village and talk to some of the artists at work in their studios. It is worth a visit if you are in the area.

Favorite Hotel in Trujillo/Huanchaco
HOTEL BRACAMONTE

This is the best hotel in the area, owned by friendly, English-speaking Juan Julio Bracamonte. Rooms are modern and there's a big pool. Breakfast is served inside or outside on the patio. You can have lunch or dinner at the hotel's good

Mud wall friezes at Huaca de la Luna, a Moche archaeological site a 30-minute drive from Trujillo.

café or walk along the beach a few blocks into town to discover other seafood restaurants.

> **ADDRESS:** Los Olivos 160, Huanchaco, near Trujillo
> www.hotelbracamonte.com
> reservas@hotelbracamonte.com.pe
> **TEL:** +51 44 461162 or +51 44 461266

Favorite Restaurant in Trujillo
CASONA DEZA CAFÉ

In a wonderful old high-ceilinged mansion, this is a place where you feel at home and comfortable. You can eat on the outdoor patio or have a drink inside and admire the contemporary artwork. The house itself is a showpiece, and it is one of my favorite places. The menu includes great pastas, pizzas, and salads.

> **ADDRESS:** Jirón Independencia 630, Trujillo
> **TEL:** +51 44 474756
> **HOURS:** Monday–Saturday, 5:30 p.m.–12 a.m.; closed Sunday

Favorite Restaurant in Huanchaco
RESTAURANTE MOCHOCO (for lunch)

> **ADDRESS:** Jiron Francisco Bolognesi, 633, Huanchaco
> **TEL:** +51 96 1343392
> **HOURS:** Tuesday–Sunday, 12:30 p.m.–3:30 p.m.; closed Monday

Favorite Hotel in Lambayeque
HOSTERIA SAN ROQUE

Retired professors from Lima restored this colonial-era home, now declared a National Monument. Rooms are clean and basic; patios are lovely with a beautiful swimming pool. It is safe, restful, and conveniently close to the Sipán museums.

> **ADDRESS:** 2 Mayo 437, Lambayeque www.hosteriasanroque.com
> hosteriasanroque@gmail.com
> **TEL:** +51 74 282860

Shipibo-Konibo

Pekon Rabi, one of a few remaining makers of *chitonti*, textiles made from homespun cotton woven on a backstrap loom. She is from a community close to the Ucayali river near Pucallpa, Peru. (www.linesoflife.xapiri.com)

People of the Shipibo-Konibo ethnic group live in the interior of north and central Peru along the Ucayali River and other Amazon tributaries. They're renowned for having extensive knowledge of medicinal plants and aesthetically sophisticated artistic traditions. The majority of the women, called Shipibas, make finely painted ceramic vessels and cotton clothing with painted or embroidered geometric patterning for both themselves and their men and boys.

These painted and embroidered textiles are so unique and culturally important that the Peruvian government declared them Cultural Heritage Patrimony. This recognition should help these beleaguered ethnic groups, often marginalized and exploited by foreign and local companies who cause deforestation, flooding, and other ecological damage through mining, logging, and palm oil cultivation on their land. Some organizations (see Resources) have excellent projects to improve living conditions and preserve cultural traditions of the indigenous Amazonian populations by encouraging artisans and by selling their skillfully-crafted artistic products.

Originally, clothes such as women's wrap skirts, wide headbands, and men's tunics were handwoven from handspun cotton, dyed with natural earth and plant dyes, and decorated by using a thin stick to paint iron-rich clay in fine, interconnected linear patterning called *kene*. Some designs relate to the four directions of the earth, others to the constellations and typical geometric forms.

LIMA

The city was founded in 1535 by Spanish conquistador Francisco Pizarro who chose a lovely setting overlooking the Pacific Ocean. The Pan-American Highway connects it to various cities along the coast, north to Ecuador and south to Chile. Including the seaport just north of the airport at Callao, Lima is the most populous city of Peru, with around 10 million people. It's also the third-largest city in the Americas, behind São Paulo and Mexico City. The National University of San Marcos is the oldest continuously functioning university in the New World, founded in Lima in 1551.

The vibrant and modern coastal city of Lima.

Today, surfers in wet suits work the waves and joggers follow paths through pretty exercise parks along the shore. Tall modern apartment buildings perch above on the cliffs. Museums full of the world's finest textiles must be perused; they are Lima's greatest treasures. Superb meals with unfamiliar ingredients from world-renowned chefs await your choice; you can head for Barranco and its famous seafood or to Miraflores for a gourmet dinner next to a 1,700-year-old adobe pyramid that was a ceremonial center, right in the middle of the city. Lima is full of surprises.

Museums

AMANO MUSEUM OF PRE-COLUMBIAN TEXTILES/*Amano Museo Textil Precolombino*

This museum was the vision of Japanese-Peruvian businessman Yoshitaro Amano (1898–1982) who passionately rescued archaeological textiles that grave robbers tossed aside in their searches for gold and ceramics. Recently, this once dark museum was revitalized by a complete renovation that doubled the exhibition space, modernized technology, and improved conservation methods. Mr. Amano's children and grandchildren now administer the museum and have opened to the public one of the most complete and spectacular collections of pre-Inca textiles in the world.

One of the galleries shows the materials and techniques used in ancient times, a display that will be fascinating to anyone interested in early or contemporary fiber work. The collection of fine Chimu cotton gauze burial shrouds is so huge that most of these breathtaking pieces remain in drawers, but you can ask the guide to open as many as you wish. The attractive displays are well lit, and the museum now hosts conferences and classes. (The Amano is not too well known by taxi drivers; help navigate with your phone perhaps.)

ADDRESS: Calle Retiro 160, Miraflores
www.museoamano.org
info@museoamano.org
TEL: +51 1 4412909
HOURS: Daily, 10 a.m.–5 p.m.
ADMISSION: 30 soles
GENERAL GUIDE: 30 soles
SPECIALIZED TEXTILE GUIDE: 50 soles (recommended)

MUSEO RAFAEL LARCO HERRERA (shortened to Larco Museum)

Pile-knotted camelid fiber cap from the Wari civilization (CE 600–1000). As the maker knotted the base of the cap, tufts of colored fiber were inserted in a specific pattern sequence in a technique much like making a miniature pile rug. From the collection of the Amano Museum.

Housed in an exquisite eighteenth-century mansion with lush gardens, this museum of pre-Columbian objects has more gold and ceramics than textiles, but the cultural-context exhibits and explanations are excellent. And the pieces that are displayed in the Textile Gallery are superb; two small tapestry fragments hold the record for the finest thread count of any textile. My favorite is the enormous 2,500-year-old Paracas mantle (a rectangular garment worn around the shoulders of a ruler). See if you can figure out how the interlocking feline-snake-bird were created before you read the label; dozens of women must have worked on this masterpiece. There are *quipus* and astonishing tapestry-woven clothing also. Be sure to see the rooms full of thousands of ceramic containers, arranged by subject like a library: people portrait pots, dog pots, llama pots, bat and snake pots, corn and potato pots—almost everything you can imagine, molded in clay as a container. The interesting Erotic Ceramics gallery is down the ramp by the café; there are signs to direct you. The gift shop and Larco Museum Café are both highly recommended. Note that the museum and café are open until 10 p.m.

ADDRESS: Av. Bolívar 1515, Pueblo Libre, Lima
www.museolarco.org
TEL: +51 1 4611312
HOURS: Daily, 9:00 a.m.–10:00 p.m.
ADMISSION: 30 soles; seniors: 25 soles
GUIDES AVAILABLE
Photos permitted without flash; no tripods or selfie sticks permitted anywhere on the premises.
HANDICAP-ACCESSIBLE throughout; free wheelchair loan, ask at the entrance.
Guide dogs for the blind are permitted.

LARCO MUSEUM CAFÉ

This is another of Gaston Acurio's successes; eat on the patio at the museum, with views of the lovely gardens.

TEL: +51 1 4611312, Ext. 207, for same-day reservations (or walk in if there is room)
cafedelmuseo@museolarco.org to request reservations in advance
HOURS: Daily, 9:00 a.m.–10:00 p.m.; last reservation at 8 p.m.

The Larco Museum Café in the lush grounds of the Museum.

NATIONAL ARCHAEOLOGY AND ANTHROPOLOGY MUSEUM

This large museum, arranged around a central garden, stores one of the best textile collections in South America. The space needs to be updated and remodeled, but a visit will nevertheless be worthwhile. Approximately 40,000 textile specimens from 500 years old (Inca) to 4,500 years old comprise the collection; naturally, it all can't be displayed at once, but there are always magnificent pieces to see. Some of the most important pieces were discovered in the dry sands of the Paracas Peninsula, by pioneering Peruvian

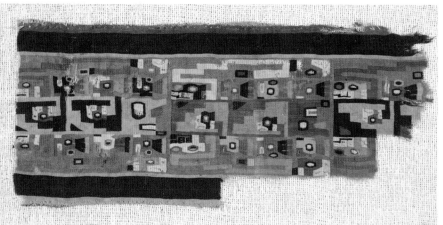

Second-finest textile in the world, made of ultrafine handspun, handwoven cotton warp with alpaca and cotton wefts. This 13" (33 cm) strip of Wari tapestry is over 1,000 years old; the colors remain bright and clear, attesting to the skill of the dyers in ancient times. Its stylized design represents anthropomorphic heads with stepped appendages tipped with the heads of birds. From the collection of the Larco Museum.

archaeologist Julio Tello between 1925 and 1928. The collection includes the knotted-string counting devices called quipus and all varieties of woven clothing and accessories: mantles, caps, and other headgear; skirts; and shirts made from or decorated with feathers, alpaca, llama, vicuña, and cotton. There is a small gift shop and café.

LOCATION: on the Plaza Bolivar, Pueblo Libre, Lima
comunicaciones-mnaahp@cultura.gob.pe
TEL: +51 3215630, Ext. 5255, or +51 6189393, Ext. 5211
HOURS: Daily, 8:45 a.m.–5:00 p.m. (last ticket sale/ entrance at 4:30)
ADMISSION: 10 soles; seniors, students, teachers, military, and disabled: 5 soles
GUIDED TOUR in English, Spanish, French, Italian, or Portuguese: 20 soles
HANDICAP-ACCESSIBLE except for one gallery; free wheelchair loan, ask at the entrance.

ANDRES DEL CASTILLO MINERAL MUSEUM/*Museo Andres del Castillo*

This museum has fabulous specimens from the bountiful mines of Peru but it's also a space full of excellent and rather unusual examples of pre-Columbian textiles. Displays showing technique add context to the actual pieces, such as the collection of coca bags called *chuspas*. The museum is housed in a beautiful old home with lots of carved wood; it has a small bookstore.

ADDRESS: Casa Belén, at Jr. De La Unión 1030, Lima
museo@mdh.com.pe
TEL: +51 1 4332831

PACHACAMAC SITE AND MUSEUM

Situated 22 miles (35 km) south of the city of Lima, overlooking the Pacific, the Pachacamac archaeological site reveals the most important religious and pilgrimage center for indigenous people 1,400 years ago. In the 1890s, archaeologists began exploring Pachacamac and found enormous mud-brick buildings and burials that had been previously looted. In one section of the site, they excavated trapezoidal temples and a large cemetery containing textile-wrapped mummy bundles of sacrificed high-status women who wove cloth for the priests. The on-site museum displays masterful ceramics and amazing textiles as well as elucidates the history and importance of the ceremonial center.

The museum is modern and excellent and the hour-long bus ride along the coast is beautiful.

Take the open-air Mirabus to the site; see bus information, page 137.

ADDRESS: Antigua Carretera Panamericana Sur Km. 31.5, Distrito de Lurín, Lima
www.pachacamac.net/
museopachacamac@cultura.gob.pe
TEL: +51 3215606 or +51 6189393, Ext. 3011
HOURS: Tuesday–Saturday, 9 a.m.–5 p.m.; Sunday, 9 a.m.–4 p.m
ADMISSION: 15 soles; students: 5 soles; seniors, military, and disabled: 50% discount; no tickets sold 45 minutes or less before closing
SPECIALIZED VISIT: 20 soles per person
GUIDED VISIT: 25 soles up to 20 people

Handwoven chuspa of alpaca fiber with warp-faced pattern stripe, from Chahuaytire, Peru.

Typical textile goods found in a stall in the Centro Artesanal Indios in Petit Thouars Street.

Crafts, Textiles, and Yarn Shopping, Miraflores

PETIT THOUARS STREET OF ARTISAN MARKETS

Dozens of complexes filled with craft stalls and souvenir shops line this street for several long blocks. Avenida Peitit Thouars joins Avenida Ricardo Palma across the street from a Dunkin' Donuts; you'll see the first big artisan signs on an orange and yellow building on the right corner. Walk along this street and with persistence, you can find any sort of handicraft or art object made anywhere in Peru. Prices are good because there is so much competition. Most places carry a mixture of alpaca rugs, straw baskets, ceramic mugs, embroidered woolen pillow covers, and other souvenirs. Some vendors sell Michell Indiecita alpaca yarn or Wildwood alpaca/silk yarns, and some places specialize in textiles. The big complex at 5245 Petit Thouars, called *Centro Artesanal Indios,* has at least three good textile-filled stalls at Numbers 23, 38, and 111. *Tienda* (shop) #38 called *Artesanía Salkantay* stocks a good variety of Andean awayos, blankets, belts, and other textiles.

If you stay at the Hostal El Patio (see page 41) in Miraflores, this craft-shopping mecca is an easy 10-minute walk away. Ask for a map at hostal reception.

AGUA Y TIERRA: Textiles and Crafts from the Amazon

Textiles and ceramics from the Amazonian basin (see page 35), look very different from anything typical of the Andean regions and this store specializes in these unusual art forms.

You will discover some stunning big pots and animal figures not found elsewhere in Lima. The owner has branched out from Amazonian art and now sells excellent quality *retablos* (boxes with little scenes inside) and woven wool pillows. The store is hard to find because signage is absent on one side and faded on the other. If you can see beyond the dark displays, there are treasures to be found.

Traditional Shipibo cloth available at Agua y Tierra.

ADDRESS: Ernesto Diez Canseco 298, across the
street from the Sheraton Hotel, Miraflores
TEL: +51 1 4446980
HOURS: Monday–Saturday, 10 a.m.–2 p.m. and
2:30 p.m.–6 p.m.

Favorite Hotel in Miraflores
HOSTAL EL PATIO
This charming hotel has twenty-three comfortable
rooms with private bathrooms, on two levels
of flower-filled patios. Three rooms are suites
with sitting room, microwave, and refrigerator.
Decorated throughout with Peruvian folk art, this
is a secure and pleasant place to stay, in a
great location. Prices are very reasonable for
this popular Miraflores neighborhood of Lima.
Cozy common areas and sunny patios with
tables and umbrellas invite conversation and
relaxation. The helpful staff speak English and
are happy to find you taxis or call for dinner
reservations. The continental breakfast is very
good, and there is free Wi-Fi. Kennedy Park,
the craft shops of Avenida Petit Thouars, and

The charming Hostal El Patio.

many excellent restaurants, such as Panchita
and SAQRA, are within walking distance. Enter
through the pretty wrought-iron gate at the front.

ADDRESS: Avenida Ernesto Diez Canseco 341,
Miraflores
www.hostalelpatio.net/
reserva@hostalelpatio.net
TEL: +51 1 4442107

Favorite Dinner Restaurants in Miraflores
PANCHITA by Gaston Acurio
Gaston just does it right, creating casual places
that serve huge portions of his special fusion
dishes. Meals start with hot bread from the round
oven over by the wall. There is a large variety of
grilled meats, Peruvian-style tamales, *anticuchos*
(skewered meats/vegetables), vegetarian choices,
a great salad bar. The waiters make you feel
welcome and will explain unusual ingredients
even though there's an English menu. Like all of
Gaston's establishments, it's upscale but not chi-
chi, stuffy, or overpriced.

ADDRESS: Calle 2 de Mayo 298, Miraflores
www.panchita.pe
reservas@panchita.com.pe
TEL: +51 1 2425957
HOURS: Sunday, noon–5:00 p.m.; Monday, noon–
11:00 p.m.; Tuesday–Saturday, noon–midnight

COSME

Cosme is a small, classy but casual place with a rainbow water-bottle ceiling. It is a real favorite for the great food made by a chef with loads of impressive credentials. The menu includes a variety of inventive dishes, ceviches, tasty sandwiches, and international combos. You can eat at regular tables or on tall chairs at friendly, long communal tables; don't be surprised if your dining neighbor hands you a clean fork to taste the dish you've just admired as it arrived at her table!

> **ADDRESS:** Tudela y Varela 160–162, San Isidro
> www.cosme.com.pe/cosme/
> reservas@cosme.com.pe
> **TEL:** +51 1 4215228
> **HOURS:** Monday–Saturday, noon–11:30 p.m.; Sunday, noon–4 p.m.

BRUJAS DE CACHICHE

The name means "witches," and in this case, charming, ethnic, bare-breasted sorcerers, which are exquisitely painted on the wall in the bar. A big, airy dining room serves generous portions of dishes with a new twist on old favorites. It is sometimes full of tables of big, noisy groups, and Lima has too many great restaurants to suffer that, so check out the bar witches, maybe stay for a pisco sour, and then get a taxi over to Cosme for dinner.

> **ADDRESS:** Calle Bolognesi 427, Miraflores (look for timbered English-style buildings on one edge of a small park)
> www.brujasdecachiche.com.pe
> reservas@brujasdecachiche.com.pe
> **TEL:** +51 1 4471833

SAQRA

The menu features creative and original dishes, beautifully presented, using the best of Peruvian seasonal ingredients. Try a salad with scallops breaded with black and white quinoa, or crispy pastries filled with carob and raisin cream, splashed with *sauco* (elderberry) sauce. The dining space is much smaller than you'll find in the other restaurant choices, but the food is equally good; the décor is quirky, fun, and casual.

> **ADDRESS:** Av. La Paz 646, Miraflores (around the corner from Hostal El Patio)
> www.saqra.pe
> saqra@saqra.pe
> **TEL:** +51 1 6508884
> **HOURS:** Monday–Thursday, noon–11:00 p.m.; Friday and Saturday, noon–midnight

The Witches of Cachiche painted on the restaurant walls. Cachiche is a community next to Ica, known for its witchcraft legends.

Favorite Lunch Restaurant
LA LUCHA SANGUCHERIA

Order huge hot sandwiches, smoothies, and other fresh drinks at the window, then sit down for a delicious and very popular Lima-style lunch or snack. You will find made-to-order fast food, good for sharing, and friendly service.

> **LOCATION:** on Diagonal 308, Miraflores. Diagonal Street is the extension of Malecón Balta (street), heading away from the ocean. From the middle of Parque Kennedy, cross Diagonal Street to the brightly lit Sangucheria window to place your order.
> **HOURS:** Daily, 7 a.m.–1 a.m.

While in this area, you should check out the **Cat Park**, an area in Parque Kennedy where fifty-plus mellow cats hang out in freedom and apparent harmony. Just walk in the pleasant park until you see lots of cats lounging about, or ask for the *parque de gatos*. Volunteers feed them and conduct a spay-neuter-adoption program.

Barranco District, Favorite Shop
ARTESANIA LAS PALLAS

In 1966, an Englishwoman named Mari came to live in balmy Lima and opened this legendary Peruvian art and handicraft store as part of her home. She's often around to explain the various pieces: where she found them, what they signify, and how they were made. The bright blue house feels like a cozy and colorful museum, but most items are for sale.

> **ADDRESS:** Cajamarca 212, Barranco
> laspallas@gmail.com
> **TEL:** +51 1 4774629
> **HOURS:** Monday–Saturday, 10 a.m.–7 p.m., or by appointment

A photograph by Mario Testino of men in traditional dress.

Favorite Barranco Museum
MATE: MARIO TESTINO MUSEUM

The museum houses two stories of stunning photographs by Peruvian artist Mario Testino, internationally renowned vanguard of fashion and portrait photography. Elaborate indigenous clothing of the Cusco region fascinated Testino and is highlighted in his crystal-clear, larger-than-life photographs, displayed in upstairs galleries. Have lunch afterwards at La Onceava, 10 minutes away by taxi.

> **ADDRESS:** Avenida Pedro de Osma 409, Barranco
> www.mate.pe/en/
> **TEL:** +51 1 2005400
> **HOURS:** Tuesday–Sunday, 10 a.m.–7 p.m.; closed Monday

Favorite Barranco Restaurant

LA ONCEAVA

This is an outdoor, casual neighborhood restaurant with a huge variety of succulent and generous seafood dishes of conch, lobster, whole fish, etc. Try the ceviche sampler (*Los Cuatro Ceviches*) or the divine *causa* sampler of crab, shrimp, and prawns layered with Peru's famous yellow potatoes, served in a little wooden boat. Live music on weekends starts around 2 p.m.

ADDRESS: Jirón San Ambrosio 420, Barranco
www.laonceava.com.pe
TEL: +51 1 2475232
WHATSAPP: 961919984
HOURS: Daily, 10:30 a.m.–5:30 p.m.

Artesania Las Pallas in the Barranco District.

Favorite Lima City Hotel
HOTEL COSTA DEL SOL WYNDHAM SALAVERRY
(not the airport hotel, but the same chain)

New in 2015, this is an excellent hotel with 144 all nonsmoking rooms and suites, spa, gym, heated outdoor pool, and fast, free Wi-Fi throughout. Contemporary décor, sleek rooms and exceptional service set this hotel apart. Located about halfway between Miraflores and the airport (30 minutes by taxi from the airport), it's in a safe and pretty residential neighborhood. And you can go downstairs for a creatively presented meal at the superb Paprika Restaurant; Limeños come just for the restaurant.

ADDRESS: Av. Salaverry 3052, Magdalena Del Mar, Lima
www.costadelsolperu.com/lima/
reservas@costadelsolperu.com
RESERVATIONS: +51 1 2009200
HOTEL: +51 1 2002300
PAPRIKA RESTAURANT: 6:00 a.m.–10:30 a.m. for breakfast buffet; noon–11 p.m. for lunch and dinner

Hand-embroidered wool pillows from Ayacucho.

HUANCAYO

Alpacas dot the mountains surrounding Huancayo.

Huancayo is a city located 100 miles (160 km) east of Lima, with a half million inhabitants who live at an altitude of 10,800 feet. Most of the attractions here are natural, like lakes, eroded stones, and glaciers. It's basically the stopping-off point for trips to smaller towns and markets in the area, but one company called Incas del Peru offers traditional crafts classes—in gourd carving, weaving, woodcarving, cooking, dance, or musical instruments. Spanish classes and homestays are also available.

There is a daily Artisans' Market (*Mercado Artesanal*) to the left of the Hotel Turismo. Vendors sell handknitted alpaca and alpaca-blend socks, gloves, and handwarmers in soft colors with detailed motifs, and also a range of acrylic sweaters and souvenirs. The Sunday market takes up ten blocks in the city center on Avenida Huancavelica. Knitted accessories are sold there, too, along with household necessities.

The towns surrounding Huancayo are much more interesting than the big city itself. You can arrange to visit any of them. Ask at your hotel (or ask locals if you speak Spanish) about patron saints' days or other holiday festivals to attend.

San Augustin de las Cajas is known for broad-brimmed felted wool hats and thick woven wall hangings, usually scenes of villages or people. The weaver uses a loosely spaced cotton thread warp and inserts half-inch thick pieces of dyed wool roving to make the images. This large-scale tapestry technique progresses faster than other tapestry, but spacing the roving evenly and blending the colors realistically takes skill. These were very popular for decades but aren't visible much in the markets nowadays. San Agustin and the nearby villages of Hualhuas, Cochas Grande, and Cochas Chico in the Mantaro Valley can be visited as day trips. Artisans make tapestries in Hualhuas and very detailed engraved gourds in the Cochas villages.

Getting to Huancayo

The comfortable Cruz del Sur buses from Lima arrive in Huancayo after a pleasant trip of about 7 hours. (See bus information on pages 136–137). There is train service from Lima to Huancayo with Ferrocarril Central Andino, but the last I heard, it only ran twice a month. It is billed as a tourist experience, but the odd schedule makes it impossible for most travelers. It is rather pricey, but there is fabulous scenery along the route. Check the website for the current schedule.

www.ferrocarrilcentral.com.pe/en_index_.php

Getting to Huancayo from Cusco on the route that looks most direct on a map is possible but not easy. The route goes right through and over the Andes and takes 2 to 3 days depending on bus schedules and road conditions (no landslides, for

A spectacular tapestry-woven wall hanging from the town of San Augustin de las Cajas.

example). Starting in Cusco, you need to go to Abancay, then Andahuaylas, north to Ayacucho, and then on to Huancayo. Much of this route has spectacular scenery, over the *puna,* or high valleys, between mountains. If you have lots of time (and don't suffer from motion sickness) and you want to see part of Peru with few tourists, this is the route for you.

Favorite Hotel in Downtown Huancayo

HOTEL TURISMO is a grand old place with huge rooms, pleasant common areas decorated with folk art weavings, and a good restaurant; book directly (English okay) for better rates. It faces the Parque Huamanmarca and the city government offices;

trufis, or collective taxis for Huancavelica leave from Ancash Street out in front.

ADDRESS: Jr. Ancash 729, Huancayo
www.turismo.hotelpresidente.com.pe
TEL: +51 64 231072

Shared taxis ply the sinuous routes to the towns surrounding Huancayo. They don't leave until they are full, which means four passengers.

Favorite Country Hotel in Huancayo
TUKI LLAJTA PUEBLO BONITO LODGE
Set on a hilltop overlooking the city and constructed of local stone, wood, and tile roofs, Tuki Llajta Lodge is a great place for relaxing in the cozy common areas or for communing with the alpacas that roam the grounds. The restaurant has a fabulous view of surrounding hills.

ADDRESS: Av. Centenario s/n, San Jerónimo de Tunán, Huancayo
http://www.tukillajta.com/
info@tukillajta.com
TEL: +51 996484554 or +51 982114500

Travel Agent in Huancayo
Cesar Delgado Acha from **Travel & Routes** is resourceful and helpful. He can find transportation for local forays to nearby village markets, or for transport onward. Travel & Routes has an office at the Cruz del Sur bus station; it is not always attended, so it is better to phone.

www.tourshuancayo.com
contacto@tourshuancayo.com
cesarturismo2008@gmail.com
TEL: +51 06422 4130 or +51 954 175 793

Incas del Peru offers day tours through craft villages around Huancayo, guided in Spanish. It's possible to go to San Jeronimo, Ingenio, and several other villages.

Here is a list of some weekly markets in the area. Ask Incas del Peru about a tour, or ask your hotel for taxi or trufi suggestions.

www.incasdelperu.org

SUNDAY: Huancayo, Jauja, Mito
MONDAY: San Agustin de Cajas
TUESDAY: Hualhuas
WEDNESDAY: San Jeronimo
THURSDAY: Sapallanga
FRIDAY: Cochas Chico (7 miles [11 km] south and great for carved gourds)
SATURDAY: Llocllapampa, Jauja

Handknitted fingerless gloves with acrylic yarn purchased from a market in Ayacucho. Maquitos, or men's arm warmers from Huancayo.

HUANCAVELICA

The Huancavelica area features rugged geography with highly varied elevation, from 6,400 feet (1,950 m) in the valleys to more than 16,000 feet (5,000 m) on snow-covered peaks. The Mantaro and other rivers flow through the valleys. The town is surrounded by dramatic, steep, forested hills, has a pretty river running through it, and has several landscaped parks. The mountains surrounding the town are the western chain of the Andes, extremely rich in mineral deposits.

In 1564, large deposits of mercury were found nearby; mercury was essential for refining silver. The Spanish Crown wasted no time in appropriating them in 1570, and by 1572, the town of Huancavelica was founded by the presumably thrilled Viceroy of Peru, Francisco de Toledo. The extraction of the quicksilver in the *socavones* (tunnels) was extremely difficult; overwork plus the toxic substance resulted in a high rate of mortality.

The Huancavelica mines were considered the greatest jewel in the crown as the mercury was used to process silver from the local mines and from as far away as the mines of Potosí in present-day Bolivia. In 1648, the Viceroy of Peru gloated that Potosí and Huancavelica were "the two pillars that support this kingdom and that of Spain." The Crown operated the mercury mines for well over 200 years until Peruvian independence in 1821. Unsurprisingly, Huancavelica remains one of the poorest cities in Peru. Indigenous peoples represent a major percentage of the population in the department and most of them are small-scale

Handknitted acrylic chullo from Huancavelica; note the typical jumping foxes motif making up the diagonal patterns.

farmers or textile producers.

Huancavelica is now a center for well-made and aesthetically pleasing knitted socks and gloves (mostly in gringo colors) fabricated for tourists.

FUN FACT:
Huancavelica has 500 to 600 genetically identified varieties of native potato!

Forty or fifty years ago there were essentially no travelers here, and the men in this area knitted distinctive accessories for themselves. Men proudly wore their arm warmers (*maquitos*) over their jacket sleeves for warmth, adornment, and regional identity. They wore chullos under their felt hats, and for special occasions, they added narrow hand-crocheted white scarves with colorful bands and dangles at the ends. Their striking arm warmers and their chullo designs are like nothing else in the country. Nowadays, women do most of the knitting and the men don't wear maquitos and chullos as often. But you can still see them at some festivals, weddings, and other events in some of the smaller towns around Huancavelica, such as Yauli.

Getting to Huancavelica

Huancayo–Huancavelica Railway: *El Tren Macho* (male, or tough, train)

The name of this historical train probably implies that it has to be strong to traverse one of the highest routes in the world. The journey from Huancayo to Huancavelica (and back) is an inexpensive, old-fashioned and enjoyable experience with a high-altitude twist: the route goes through thirty-eight tunnels and over fifteen bridges. Chugging slowly along in the rarefied air, the diesel-drawn train takes 5 to 6 hours to cover the distance of 80 miles (129 km) between the two towns. Part of the route follows the Mantaro River through rocky, uninhabited countryside that you can't see any other way, and in the highest parts, it's stunning. I recommend it for the experience but also because a car or bus twists through the mountain roads until you are green.

El Tren Macho runs back and forth every other day. It departs Huancayo for Huancavelica at 6:30 a.m. on Monday, Wednesday, and Friday, arriving around noon. It returns from Huancavelica on Tuesday and Thursday (and perhaps Saturday) at 6:30 a.m. and arrives in Huancayo 5 or 6 hours later. It is best to buy tickets the day before at the station. Note that there may be another, less interesting, AutoWagon train running; you want the Tren Macho.

BUS OR TAXI

BY BUS: Lima–Pisco–Huancavelica: 310 miles (499 km), 11 to 12 hours

Lima–Huancayo–Huancavelica: 276 miles (444 km), about 9 hours

FROM HUANCAYO, take a local bus or a faster shared taxi (or private, which costs more) to Huancavelica, about 4 hours away. Transportation leaves from the main plaza in front of the Hotel Turismo.

Shopping

There are several artisan collectives and fair-trade organizations operating out of Huancavelica and its surrounding towns.

QAMPAQ ARTE/*Arte hecho para ti* or *Art for You*

This is a fair-trade establishment that sells knitwear made by women from the rural community of Ccochaccasa. They formed the Asociación de Artesanas Makyss and create a large variety of scarves and sweaters in soft alpaca with modern, wearable designs.

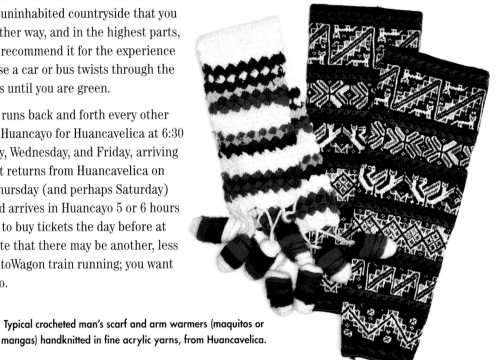

Typical crocheted man's scarf and arm warmers (maquitos or mangas) handknitted in fine acrylic yarns, from Huancavelica.

ADDRESS: Jiron Arica 230 (near the museum)
HOURS: Monday–Friday, 10 a.m.– 8 p.m.;
Saturday, 9 a.m.–1 p.m.

Markets

Shoppers at the Huancavelica Sunday market, using dark handwoven lliqllas under horizontally striped mantas to carry produce and other market purchases.

Sunday is the big market day in Huancavelica, and the town is so small that it's easy to find the colored tarps set up all along the river that flows through town. This used to be a great place to see local men wearing unusual knitted arm warmers and distinctive chullos, but nowadays, the markets at Yauli and smaller towns and villages are a better bet. Older women in Huancavelica continue to wear handwoven mantas or llicllas and typical skirts, but on my 2018 trip, I didn't see any men in traditional accessories at this market or elsewhere in town. But for local festivals, men do wear finely knitted arm warmers, socks, and chullos with motifs of jumping foxes (see chullo, page 48) among the more common designs.

The permanent daily market on Jr. Victor Garma has some typical accessories such as chullos, pom-pom ties, and crocheted scarves at stalls 58

and 59; otherwise, the market is an assortment of foods, meats, and factory-made clothes. Handicrafts are sold on the north side of the Plaza de Armas and also under the blue arches of the Municipalidad Provincial. Alpaca or alpaca-blend socks are very popular in the street markets. There's a collection of kiosks underneath the Parque Ramon Castillo where a friendly woman named Giorgina sold me some finely knitted arm warmers and a chullo, but this is one of the few places I found in Huancavelica that sold excellent-quality traditional knitted items; I'm not sure if they are not being made much anymore or if the tourists are not interested in buying them, so the knitters just make them for their own use.

Nearby Yauli has a bustling Saturday market. Women from Yauli come to Huancavelica with their knitted goods to sell on Avenida Muñoz near the Plaza de Armas.

Favorite Hotel in Huancavelica
HOTEL VICTORIA
The rooms are basic (some with a nice view of the church in back) and very clean with hot water, and the staff is friendly. Book directly for the best prices. You can eat at the good rotisserie chicken restaurant down the street on the left. Ask the girl at the hotel desk where it is or for a recommendation.

ADDRESS: Manco Capac 371, Huancavelica (Esquina Plaza de Armas)
TEL: +51 67 452954

The competition, **Hotel Presidente**, is in a nice old stone building on the main plaza, but it is very expensive for plain-walled rooms with vintage (not in a good sense) bedspreads.

AYACUCHO

This pretty town of about 180,000 lies in a sunny fertile valley in south-central Peru. The elevation of 9,007 feet (2,746 m) makes Ayacucho warmer and more pleasant than many other highland towns. In 1824, the Battle of Ayacucho decided freedom for the indigenous revolutionaries from the royalists in the Latin-

Sheep's wool and alpaca pillow cover embroidered with stylized Moche warriors by Ayacucho artist Richard Albites.

American wars of independence. Victory here freed the country of Peru and ensured the independence of the other South American republics from Spain.

In the 1970s and 1980s, Ayacucho was the base for terror campaigns against the government and other factions by the revolutionary organization Shining Path. Abimael Guzmán Reynoso, a philosophy professor at the National University in Ayacucho, founded the movement in 1970 as an offshoot of the Communist Party of Peru. Guzmán was tried and imprisoned for life, and the ill-conceived movement has long been squelched. Ayacucho is now peaceful and a beautiful place to visit. Easter week celebrations and religious processions are more fervent and lively here than anywhere else, perhaps because of its unfortunate history and because this city has thirty-three churches. The city is also known for its folk handicrafts. Artisans in Ayacucho are renowned for textile specialties, mainly embroidery and tapestry weaving.

Getting to Ayacucho

The half-dozen round-trip flights on LC Peru or LATAM to and from Lima cost around US$140 to $170.

Cruz del Sur buses all leave and return to Lima at night, and cost $52 one-way for best class. The bus lurches through the dark Andean mountain passes and switchbacks for 10 hours; go in the daytime if you can, or pay more to fly over the landscape. On the Ayachucho–Lima route, Molina Bus Company's VIP class only travels at night, but there are several morning departures of other classes that look very good also. See bus information, page 136.

Shopping

Most textile and folk artists have stalls at the **Artisans' Market (*Mercado de Artesania*)** near the jail; it's the best place to shop for embroidered hangings, pillows, and purses. There are a number of interesting workshops around the perimeter of Plaza Santa Ana, including the Gallardo tapestry workshop.

The Shosaku Nagase Handicraft Market at Maravillas 101 is a great place to look for local artisans' weavings and other treasures such as colorful retablos—intricate scenes of little molded figures inside a box with doors that close to protect the contents. Originally, these were portable or traveling altars and contained a saint or a nativity scene, but nowadays, artists create all sorts of scenes such as picking cactus fruit, making felt hats, or weaving.

Favorite Hotel in Ayacucho
HOTEL SANTA ROSA

Originally constructed in 1630 as a mansion for a Spanish governor, it was renovated in 1972, and declared a historical monument in 1991. Peaceful and quiet rooms border a large central patio with tables and umbrellas. It is in a good location with reasonable room rates.

> **ADDRESS:** Jr. Lima 166, Ayacucho
> www.hotelsantarosa.com.pe
> informes@hotelsantarosa.com.pe
> hotel_santa_rosa@yahoo.es
> **TEL:** +51 66 314614

Favorite Restaurant in Ayacucho
VIAVIA CAFÉ AYACUCHO

Overlooking the Plaza de Armas, and serving real coffees, this place is a gem. The alpaca burger gets consistent great reviews, but I don't eat the creatures that give me my sweaters! They also have quinoa-encrusted trout, vegetarian options, and desserts. The restaurant is part of the good ViaVia Hotel.

> **ADDRESS:** Portal Constitucion 4, Plaza de Armas, Ayacuch
> www.viavia.world/en/south-america/ayacucho
> ayacucho@viavia.world
> **TEL:** +51 66 312834

Hand-embroidered wool pillows are characteristic of Ayacucho and widely available in artisan markets.

CUSCO

Cusco's designation as a UNESCO World Heritage site in 1983, just as it was becoming a popular tourist destination, saved its authenticity by mandating preservation and restoration of structures in the historic center of town. Only limited changes have since been allowed, maintaining edifices and requiring the aesthetically important red tile roofs and whitewashed buildings.

The famed ancient Andean city of Cusco is a wonderful place to discover a wide array of Peruvian textiles.

Cusco was built under the Inca ruler Pachacutec into a complex urban center, but when the Spaniards conquered it in the sixteenth century, they built Baroque churches and palaces right over the ruins of the Inca city. Walls of meticulously cut granite underlie Spanish Baroque churches and other colonial structures in and around the main Plaza de Armas.

If you don't think too much about that aspect of it, Cusco is charming, gorgeous, breathtaking, and very touristic. It's a delightful place to visit, stay for a festival or two, buy some textiles, have superb meals, and absorb the ancient culture. It is a very safe city, thanks to troops of friendly police patrolling the streets and English speakers are easy to find. Shopping offers something for everyone —from the most traditional heritage textile to items made especially for tourists.

However, UNESCO says, "[N]ew tourism development is threatening the preservation and functional capacity of ancient buildings, which in some cases are altered or replaced by new buildings for tourism and trade, relocating the original dwellers to the periphery."

Getting to Cusco from Lima

As usual for crossing mountain ranges, you have your choice of a long winding bus ride or a quick flight. Flights cost about twice as much as a modern tourist bus and save lots of time if your schedule is tight. There are dozens of daily flights from Lima. The cheap and excruciatingly slow local bus travels over the Andes for 3 days if you have more time than money. Whatever kind of bus you decide on, choose a morning departure so you can see the breathtaking mountain vistas. See page 136 for transportation info.

Getting to Cusco from Puno

Comfortable and modern tourist buses of the Inca Express company ply the spectacular highland route from Cusco to Puno and back, edging Lake Titicaca for a while and then puffing over the 14,000-foot pass at La Raya and on down to Cusco. Inca Express also has a good bus tour that includes a buffet lunch and the most interesting sights along this route, such as the Inca two-story temple at Raqchi.

www.incaexpress.com/
reservas@Incaexpress.com
CUSCO OFFICE: 084 634838; +51 984 705301
PUNO OFFICE: +51 365654; +51 951304037

The PeruRail Titicaca train runs to Cusco from Puno on Wednesday, Friday, and Sunday. The trip takes 10½ hours, but it's a mellow, entertaining way to travel. The updated train includes a good restaurant and observation cars. Bring warm clothes; a book, tablet, or your knitting; snacks and water or drinks. There is also a luxury sleeper train called the Belmond Andean Explorer that does the same route in a couple of days for about $1,300.

www.perurail.com/trains/perurail-titicaca/

Shopping

CENTER FOR TRADITIONAL TEXTILES OF CUSCO/*Centro de Textiles Tradicionales del Cusco*

Begun in 1996 by the dynamic Nilda Callañaupa Alvarez, the *Centro de Textiles Tradicionales del Cusco* (CTTC) empowers textile artists through encouraging creative but quality work, and through effective marketing. The nonprofit center enables weavers to maintain their identity and textile traditions while improving their quality of life. Nilda is from Chinchero, a Quechua weaving village about an hour from Cusco, and thus is the best possible resource to guide the weavers and knitters to success. CTTC programs to motivate young weavers are popular in the villages and help to teach them textile techniques as well as organization skills.

At the Cusco Center, weavers from different communities demonstrate their work while you watch. The walls are hung with exquisite woven pieces from the ten project villages; all work is for sale at prices that make weaving worthwhile for the artisans. Take a look around at the gorgeous textiles, then for an appreciation of craftsmanship and price, watch the weavers as they pick up pattern threads and send the shuttle across, progressing one thin strand at a time!

An excellent small museum called "Weaving Lives" gives textile context with explanations of village traditions, textile techniques, motifs, dyestuffs, and more. All of Nilda's good textile books are available at the Center, too.

ADDRESS: Avenida del Sol 603, next to Koricancha Temple, Cusco
www.textilescusco.org
TEL: +51 84 228117 or 236880
HOURS: Daily before 7:30 a.m.–8 p.m.
FREE ADMISSION

CENTER FOR WEAVERS OF CHINCHERO/*Awayricch'Arichiq*

Visitors learning about natural dyeing from Nilda and weavers from the CTTC at the weaving center in Chinchero.

It is also possible to visit the Center's Chinchero textile site to see people weaving, spinning, and knitting outdoors in the central courtyard. Many varieties of the exquisite Chinchero-style woven textiles are sold here, such as lliqllas (carrying cloths for babies and other cargo), purses, belts, knitted chullos, and large ponchos. Pretty knitted sweaters are also available here. This is one of the ten village workshops that provides the woven and knitted pieces sold in the CTTC in Cusco. Nilda says the "principal objectives of the weavers of Chinchero are to weave the ancient patterns of the area, revive the use of natural dyes, to reintroduce traditional dress . . . and commercialize high quality textiles to generate a sustainable income."

It's more fun to visit Chinchero weavers on a Sunday when the weekly market takes place one block from the weaving center. You can get a taxi from Cusco and also visit the Maras salt basins and Moray, to see the circular Inca agricultural terraces.

Ask about day trips to Chinchero at CTTC on Avenida Sol.

ADDRESS: Calle Manzanares, Chinchero
TEL: +51 84 228117 or 236880 (call ahead)

AWANA KANCHA/Textile Palace

Better known for the "petting zoo" than the textile shop, this place has alpacas, llamas, and vicuñas in large enclosures near the pathway so you can feed and sometimes pet them. It's the perfect place for animal photo ops—and kids. Begun as a nonprofit association to keep Andean weaving techniques alive, Awana Kancha offers employment in the textile realm to improve quality of life for the population. Village women demonstrate fiber processing, dyeing, and weaving, and get a fair price for their work. The very high-quality and unique products are pricey but beautiful, especially the tapestries.

ADDRESS: Km. 23 Carretera Cusco-Pisac, Cusco
www.awanakancha.com
TEL: +51 84 632990

A Maximo Laura tapestry woven with traditional Andean methods produces a gorgeous contemporary design.

MUSEO MAXIMO LAURA

More a gallery than a museum, this space showcases the bold, colorful tapestries designed by the talented yet generous and humble weaver Maximo Laura. Laura's goal is to revive ancient methods while staying true to his contemporary creative vision of beautifully shaded, abstracted shapes. He says he often dreams of wild tapestry configurations and figures. Nowadays, a crew of several dozen weavers carries out his unique designs in his Lima workshop. Laura is also known internationally, with his tapestries appearing in the Smithsonian's collections and at UNESCO headquarters.

He has earned many awards, including "National Living Treasure of Peru," following UNESCO guidelines to distinguish an artist whose role is to preserve and elevate the culture of their homeland. His tapestry technique brings the usual flat tapestry to a new dimension, with warp and weft wrapping and embroidered details for texture and dimension. He blends wool yarn colors for extra subtlety and weaves shapes within shapes for some very striking work. See below for textile workshops with Maximo Laura.

ADDRESS: Calle Santa Catalina Ancha 304, Cusco (on the corner, a few doors away from Incanto Restaurant)
www.museomaximolaura.com
info@maximolaura.com
TEL: +51 84 227383
HOURS: Monday–Saturday, 9:30 a.m.–8 p.m.; Sunday, 5 p.m.–8 p.m.

TEXTIL SULCA

The store and gallery feature innovative tapestries by Walter Sulca and family.

Skillfully woven alpaca tapestries that appear three-dimensional with pre-Hispanic motifs in the undulating curves were started by earlier generations of the Sulca family weavers from Ayacucho. Lesser-known weavers copy their configurations. Sulca artisans also make and sell small pieces here with embroidered ancient motifs from Paracas and other locations. **Textil Sulca Huayllarccoca** is a second and larger complex of the same name outside of town, with a tapestry gallery, weaving demonstrations, and furry animals to observe. This operation is in a large rust-red building by the side of the road outside of Cusco on the way to Tambomachay, in Communidad Huayllarccoca. It is easy to visit on the same day you see Sacsahuayman. Taxi drivers know the place.

www.sulcatextiles.com.pe
artexaperu@gmail.com
TEL: +51 930717897 or
+51 931260197

Top: Rolls of golons, handwoven skirt trim, for sale in Cusco markets.
Below: Three bundled core grass baskets and a handspun, hand-knotted xicra bag of chambira palm fiber, from the Iquitos area of the Amazon River Basin.

MARKET CENTERS FOR CRAFTS AND TEXTILES

Often you'll stick your head in a doorway to find a cluster of shops and vendors selling textiles and handicrafts. One such center is up Triunfo Street from the cathedral about a block on the right, called **Artesanias Yachaywasi.** Inside on the left side is a helpful woman named Luisa who has a great collection of oldish ponchos and awayos from all over the Andes of Peru.

XAPIRI/Indigenous Arts from the Amazon Rainforest

This fair-trade store offers embroidered and painted cotton textiles as well as baskets and ceramics from the indigenous Shipibo-Konibo communities of the Amazon. They were showing a film series about the Amazon when I was there last; if you go, see if any posters for films are pasted on the door. On the store website, there's a very interesting series of photos and explanations of ancestral Shipibo-Konibo textile traditions—cotton weaving and painting of the traditional cloth—that Xapiri store owners want to revive.

ADDRESS: Calle Garcilaso 210, Cusco (off Plaza Regocijo)
www.linesoflife.xapiri.com
www.xapiri.com
peace@xapiri.com
TEL: +51 84 596435
HOURS: Daily, 8:30 a.m.–8:30 p.m.

Favorite Cusco Restaurants

Cusco has more great restaurants than the average traveler will have time for.

CHICHA

The new star in town is Chicha, another of renowned chef Gaston Acurio's creations. Remarkably affordable, relaxed, and casual, Chicha is a block off the main plaza, upstairs in an atmospheric house with open vaulted ceilings. The innovative dishes show Gaston's twist on traditional food with native ingredients.

ADDRESS: 261 Plaza Regicijo, Cusco (around the block from Hotel Marqueses)
reservacionescusco@chicha.com.pe
TEL: +51 84 240520 or 84 240717
HOURS: Daily, noon–10:30 p.m.

MORENA RESTAURANT

Also called Morena Peruvian Kitchen, this is a comfortable, modern and classy restaurant with delicious food and innovative presentations and excellent drinks. It gets rave reviews everywhere.

ADDRESS: 348-B Calle Plateros, right off the Plaza de Armas, Cusco
TEL: +51 84 437832
HOURS: Daily, noon–10 p.m.; no reservations

Mother with baby wrapped in a handwoven manta.

CICCIOLINA

This restaurant offers an appealing bar area for casual drinks and tapas and a larger room for dining on dishes such as their divine butternut squash raviolis. Go through the big door (off Calle Triunfo) into a colonial patio and up the stairs; the restaurant is beautiful inside.

ADDRESS: Calle Triunfo 393, Cusco (inside courtyard and upstairs)
TEL: +51 84 239510
HOURS: Daily, 8–11 a.m., 12–3 p.m., and 6–10 p.m.

MARCELO BATATA'S

Around the corner is Marcelo Batata's, with beautifully presented, contemporary Peruvian cuisine. The menu includes many alpaca specialties, twists on typical combinations, and interesting vegetarian dishes.

ADDRESS: Calle Palacio 121, Cusco (upstairs)
reservas@cuscodining.com
TEL: +51 84 222424 or 984115597
HOURS: Daily, 12:30 p.m.–11 p.m.

PUCARA

If you are low on energy and want a simple meal, the small and casual Pucara (since 1988) offers comforting typical Peruvian soups and other dishes. The menu comes with helpful photos.

ADDRESS: Calle Plateros 309, Cusco
TEL: 84 222027
HOURS: Daily, noon–10 p.m.

INCANTO RESTAURANT and GREENS RESTAURANT

Just off the Plaza de Armas, to the left of the cathedral are Incanto (downstairs) and Greens (upstairs). Owned by the same company, these two excellent places serve Peruvian favorites, Italian cuisine, and fusion dishes. The larger Incanto has atmospheric Inca granite walls, a full-view glass-fronted kitchen, and a pizza oven. Greens is more casual with equally delicious salads and other organic dishes, and a wonderful breakfast.

ADDRESS: Santa Catalina Angosta 139, Cusco
reservas@cuscorestaurants.com
TEL: + 51 84 254753 or 84 243379
INCANTO: Daily, 11:30 a.m.–11 p.m.
GREENS: Daily, 8 a.m.–11 p.m.

Greens Restaurant offers great organic dishes and a convenient location.

Quintana, has a program to keep street boys in school; he takes them to soccer games and gives them breakfast every Saturday at the hotel. You can bring gently used kid clothes and backpacks to donate. Hotel Marqueses is affiliated with the trustworthy SAS Travel; see below.

ADDRESS: 265 Garcilaso Street, Cusco (half a block from Plaza Regocijo)
www.marqueseshotel.com/
TEL: +51 84 264249 or 84 257819
reservas@hotelmarqueses.com

Favorite Hotel in Cusco
HOTEL MARQUESES

Two blocks off the Plaza de Armas you will find this safe and centrally located heritage hotel, built in the late 1700s. The charming courtyard with Spanish fountain has chairs and tables for relaxing or eating breakfast. Rooms are comfortable and atmospheric with thick stone walls and typical hand-hewn beam ceilings. Buffet breakfast is included, and there is a free airport shuttle. English is spoken and you can book directly by email. The wonderful owner, Dr.

Favorite Travel and Tour Agency
SAS TRAVEL

ADDRESS: Calle Garcilaso 270, Cusco
www.incatrailperutrek.com
info@sastravelperu.com
reservas@sastravelperu.com
TEL: +51 84 249194
HOURS: Daily, 8 a.m.–8 p.m.; closed Sunday

This efficient and helpful travel company with great English-speaking staff can get your Machu Picchu train and entrance tickets in advance—or plan an amazing choice of other Peru adventures, such as a Pisac market visit, an Inca Trail hike, a Mt. Salcantay trek, or an Amazon jungle macaw-watching trip.

Sacred Valley of the Incas

The 70-mile expanse of verdant farm fields and ancient Inca terraces running along the Urubamba River from Cusco to Machu Picchu is known as the Sacred Valley. It includes the highland towns of Ollantaytambo and Pisac, home to significant Inca ruins as well as bustling market places offering the gamut of textiles. For my tour groups, we now land at the Cusco airport from Lima and go directly to lower altitude of the Sacred Valley. Spending the first night there makes acclimation to high altitude much easier. You can stay either in the sweet little town of Ollantaytambo, 2 hours northwest of Cusco at "only" 9,432 feet (2,875 m) altitude, or in Urubamba, at the same altitude and about 1½ hours from Cusco.

OLLANTAYTAMBO

EL ALBERGUE OLLANTAYTAMBO HOTEL

Owned by American Wendy Weeks, El Albergue is conveniently right at the Machu Picchu train station. Trains don't travel at night, so your sleep will be peaceful. You can get up in the morning, have an espresso and breakfast, and hop right on the train to Machu Picchu. El Albergue is a historic and romantic hotel whose beautiful rooms have high-beamed ceilings, wooden floors, and a crisp modern aesthetic. The hotel can arrange airport pickup and tours/guides to Machu Picchu; you can also leave your large suitcases here while you take a small bag to Machu Picchu.

www.elalbergue.com
reservations@elalbergue.com
TEL: +51 84 204014 or +51 954151823

SACRED DREAMS LODGE

The beautiful lodge rooms and buildings blend harmoniously with the environment, showing "great respect for Pacha Mama" says their website. Constructed of local, traditional, and ecological materials of adobe, clay, stone, and wood, this pleasant place is perfect for relaxing and acclimating after your international flight. There is even a small swimming pool. Transport from Cusco Airport and to Machu Picchu train station (30 minutes) is available. Book on the website for best prices

ADDRESS: Tacllancca-Pumahuanca, Urubamba, Peru
http://sacred-dreams-lodge.com.

LA CAPILLA LODGE

This is a less expensive and more rustic version of the other hotels recommended in this area, and it has rave reviews.

Rumichaca Km. 72 Carretera Ollantaytambo, Urubamba
www.capillalodge.com
capillareservations@gmail.com
TEL: +51 84 434627 or +51 91 4844962

Inkayni Peru Tours receives rave reviews for their private day tours of the Sacred Valley, Ollantaytambo, Pisac, and Machu Picchu. Some trips also include the weaving complex at Chinchero so you can witness the demonstrations of natural dyeing and ancient weaving techniques. Guests typically comment that they felt the guide was "a friend sharing his community," instead of a tour guide.

Centro Artesanal Arte Inka, Triunfo Street 392, Office 214, Ollantaytambo
info@inkayniperutours.com
reservations@inkayniperutours.com
TEL: +51 084 597097
WHATSAPP: +51 979858544 or +51 964180948
HOURS: Monday–Saturday 9 a.m.–7 p.m.; Sunday 4 p.m.–7 p.m.

A market stall in Ollantaytambo sells a variety of textiles from all over Peru.

PISAC

MUSEO INKARIY

In the Sacred Valley, on the road between Urubamba and Pisac, be sure to take time to visit the wonderful, innovative **Inkariy Museum** that focuses on pre-Hispanic peoples and their cultures. The visionary project opened in 2015 after 13 years of work by the talented Merida family of Cusco. Their vision is to show Andean highlanders their proud cultural heritage and to exhibit for all the important pre-Columbian societies in an entertaining, modern manner— no boring didactic panels in this museum. The Meridas decided to collaborate with the most talented "outsider" in the business, Peruvian Bruno Meneses Alva, now curator at the Amano Museum in Lima. Bruno's museum experience and his research on pre-Columbian iconography were paramount to the design because the figures that the Meridas formed accurately reflect the body type, clothing, and accessories of each culture.

Merida family members sculpted all the ultra-realistic display mannequins for each of the nine cultural scenes and did the videography and music. The displays are an overview of the most important pre-Hispanic cultures in separate halls for each: Caral, Chavín, Paracas, Moche, Nazca, Wari, Lambayeque, Chimu, and Inca. It's a further reminder that the Inca were at the end of centuries of other cultures whose inventions and discoveries they enlarged upon. You can ask for a guide or go through

on your own. There is also a café for lunch and drinks.

ADMISSION: 35 soles
ADDRESS: Main road between Pisac and Urubamba, just outside the town of Calca; kilometer 53
www.museoinkariy.com/en
reservas@museoInkariy.com
TEL: +51 84 792819
HOURS: Daily, 9 a.m.–5 p.m.

PISAC HANDICRAFTS MARKET

Every year, this market spreads out along more side streets, with stalls and vendors selling loads of the same items you will see in Cusco. Shops line the streets along the market area, too; I have occasionally found some textile treasures in them, like old knitted caps or chullos. The advantage here is the sheer amount of choice in a small area. You might find the perfect color combo of embroidered pillow or the sweater that fits perfectly. Sunday is best because more vendors come into town from other areas, but more tourists also arrive. Many vendors also sell their wares around the plaza on Tuesday and Thursday.

SAS Travel does all-day tours that include the Pisac market, the very impressive Pisac archaeological site, and the weaving village of Chinchero for a reasonable US$25. Go on Tuesday, Thursday, or Sunday for the best market days; you have your choice of climbing the Pisac ruins or staying below to shop; the guide will find you later.

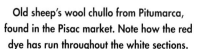

Old sheep's wool chullo from Pitumarca, found in the Pisac market. Note how the red dye has run throughout the white sections.

MACHU PICCHU

Everybody knows Machu Picchu as the stone buildings with views of green mountains, the Inca sanctuary or retreat, or something else. Nobody is sure what it was used for and who really lived there, but it's on everyone's bucket list to visit; it's a National Park and a UNESCO World Heritage site. Basically, everybody agrees that it is a stunning, unforgettable, mind-boggling site. As such, it is getting more popular every year and the National Park officials are wisely restricting access by having two shifts of visitors daily. One could also say visiting is getting more complicated and more regimented. Go sooner rather than later.

First of all, I recommend spending the night in Machu Picchu Village (formerly the town of Aguas Calientes) to be able to experience the site with a minimum of other tourists. (See Machu Picchu Village hotel information on pages 65–66.)

There are many pages of advice online about visiting Machu Picchu, but remember to take plenty of cash in both dollars and soles. Tickets (if you didn't buy them earlier), shuttle bus tickets, and so forth all require cash payments. There are a few ATMs but with a captive audience in a tiny space, they are often empty.

Chullos for sale at the modern Machu Picchu market.

Getting to Machu Picchu

There are two choices for the train, a longer or shorter route, depending on where you board. You can get on the train at Poroy, only 25 minutes out of Cusco by taxi; that choice entails a 3½- to 4-hour train ride, or you can take a bus or shared taxi to the Ollantaytambo train station and get to Machu Picchu in 1½ hours. (There is also the wildly expensive Hiram Bingham Luxury Express at around US$500 one way. Write and tell me about it if you ride on it.) Two train companies, PeruRail and Inca Rail, haul tourists to Machu Picchu many times daily; both have similar prices and similar clean, modern cars. The trains and service are very good on PeruRail; I haven't tried Inca Rail but their website is easier to navigate.

The websites are self-explanatory; decide when you want to leave and from which departure point, and then choose convenient train schedules. Train ticket prices vary according to departure times and train type, from US$55 to $115 each way, including a drink and a snack. PeruRail's least expensive Expedition class train is absolutely fine, with big windows, luggage racks, bathroom, and

snacks. The ride along the river is beautiful; if you have a choice, get a seat on the left side of the train heading to Machu Picchu. If you buy online, you don't get a choice of seats, but if you buy your tickets in Lima or Cusco (see website for sales points), you can choose seating. I prefer to buy train tickets ahead of time since Machu Picchu is so very popular now, and I want to make sure I am on the train on the correct date.

www.incarail.com
www.perurail.com

If you want to make it easy on yourself, email David or Irwin at SAS Travel for tickets before you travel. Let them know what you need and when, and they will get your train and site entrance tickets for you ahead of time. For a reasonable price, SAS will deliver you in a van to your Urubamba hotel or to Ollantaytambo to get on the train and they will pick you up when you return. Stay next door at the Hotel Marqueses, and your tickets will be delivered to your room or you can drop by the SAS office near Plaza Regocijo.

Shopping
MACHU PICCHU MARKET

Once you get off the train, you'll pass through the station and down a little pathway to waiting hotel reps. (Most hotels will send someone to help with your luggage and maneuver the route to the hotel if you have emailed ahead with your arrival times.) Continue out the gate and conveniently right into the enormous Artisans' Market. Your hotel will be either uphill or downhill through the market from here, but in any case on this introductory walk you'll be overwhelmed by the number of stalls full of textiles, T-shirts, and tchotchkes. Later, after you have seen the famous Inca site, you can come

Embroidered pillow covers from Ayacucho with contemporary swirl and circle designs.

A modern stall at the Machu Picchu market offers textiles and accessories from all of Peru.

back to pore over the stalls. There's something for everyone, including more iconic mountain/jungle themed T-shirts than you thought possible— good presents in pink size six months up to triple XL.

Like the Pisac Sunday market, the advantage here is the sheer quantity and quality to choose from. For some reason vendors in this market offer a great variety of alpaca on wool hand-embroidered wall-hangings, pillow covers, and small zippered purses from the Ayacucho area. I often find a colorful new pillow that I can't resist. In recent years the designs have evolved from flowers and tendrils to contemporary circles, dots, and swirls. New to this market are several modern stalls with walls and overhead lighting that are like mini-stores, selling fine alpaca machine-knitted goods such as sweaters, armwarmers, scarves, and caps. Thanks to computerized knitting machines, many of these are patterned with fine geometrics in dozens of color combinations and are very attractive.

Sometimes finely knitted chullos with a profusion of thick multicolored tassels and diamond patterns traced in white seed beads (from the Ocongate area) can be found here; an example

with very fine gauge with no damage can cost at least US$100, and I think well worth it. A recent rather slap-dash chullo version has couched patterns of larger white seed beads, and brightly-colored (mostly red) medium-gauge knitting underneath. These could be worn or used as wall decorations but they are not traditional. Tapestry-woven wall hangings of varying quality from the Huancayo region and embroidered panels and pillows from the Uros Islands drape the walls of many stalls. I've already mentioned the little figures composed from ancient textile shards sold here that we shouldn't buy. Rocks and minerals are big items here, too, and most specimens really are from Peru's Andean mines. Save some time in your Machu Picchu schedule to wander this interesting market; perhaps you'll find the perfect souvenir or present.

Favorite Hotels at Machu Picchu Village

HOTEL WAMAN

This hotel is a two- to three-block walk from the train station, and it's worth every step. The place is new, modern, and very classy in a comfortable

Elders in ceremonial dress at a festival in Ollantaytambo.

way, all wood and glass with soaring ceilings and stunning jungle views in all directions. Rooms are not huge, but they are sleek and nicely decorated. Common areas are pleasant, and there's a great coffee bar. Breakfast is bountiful and starts at 4:30 a.m. for those who want to be on the first shuttle bus to the site. The restaurant is very good, and the hotel is also near other good restaurants. Email the helpful hotel staff for reservations. If you ask, they will meet you at the train and help you with luggage. The hotel provides free luggage storage while you visit the ruins.

ADDRESS: Calle Wiracocha 202, Machu Picchu Village
reservas@wamanhotels.com
TEL: +51 84 211234 or +51 84 223533

HATUN INTI BOUTIQUE MACHU PICCHU

If you want a place closer to the buses to Machu Picchu and downhill from the train station, check out the newly renovated Hatun Inti Boutique.

There are two hotels named Hatun Inti in town; choose this boutique hotel that is downhill from the train station, right at the bottom of the artisan market's stairs. (The Classic is fine, too, but not in such a convenient location.) Hatun Inti Boutique is between the roaring river and the local train tracks, but don't worry, it's not noisy because very few trains go by. This one is a splurge compared to Hotel Waman; you pay for the convenient location. Rooms are comfortable and chic, with big windows that overlook the river and the wall of greenery across the flow. Obviously, the train station will be an uphill walk the next day, through the crafts stalls.

ADDRESS: Avenida Imperio de los Incas 606, Machu Picchu Village
www.grupointi.com
www.hatuninti.com
reservas@grupointi.com for reservations
hoteles@hatuninti.com
TEL: +51 84 234312 or +51 84 242037

Favorite Restaurants in Machu Picchu Village

INDIO FELIZ

This is an excellent place to eat. A Frenchman and his Peruvian wife moved to Machu Picchu Village and started Indio Feliz decades ago. I keep going back for the food and the cozy fireplace surrounded by larger-than-life naked ladies sculpted from granite, part of the casual and kitsch décor. The atmosphere is warm and friendly, with fabulous drinks and food such as pepper chicken with Peruvian pisco sauce, and orange tart with custard sauce and ice cream. It's a bit hard to find; go to the plaza with the statue of Pachacutec. Face the church and walk right, up the street a block or two. Indio Feliz is down a little lane on the left side with clear signage.

ADDRESS: Calle Lloque Yupanqui, Machu
Picchu Pueblo
www.indiofeliz.com
reservas@indiofeliz.com
TEL: +51 84 211090 or 211320 for
reservations (or make reservations on the
website)
HOURS: Daily, noon–10 p.m.

FULL HOUSE PERUVIAN CUISINE

Close to the Hatun Inti Hotel, the restaurant
features a casual atmosphere and good food
with a pizza oven that turns out bubbly hot
rounds. The windows look out on the wild
river, and there are a few outside tables on a
narrow balcony.

ADDRESS: Av. Imperio De Los Incas 620,
Aguas Calientes, Machu Picchu Village
TEL: +51 84 314051
HOURS: Daily, 10:30 a.m.–10 p.m.

TOTO'S HOUSE

The restaurant is in a two story tile-roofed
house that you can't miss, right by the
bridge on the way to the buses. It serves
delicious food including à la carte Italian
pizzas and Peruvian favorites. You'll be
comfortable if you can get a dinner table by
the cozy round fireplace which also serves
as a small grill for some dishes. The center
tables are often occupied by huge groups
who eat at the buffet. It has a good view of
the river if it's daylight, and there is a good
coffee bar near the street, with outside
tables. Toto's is to the right of Hatun Inti
Hotel and owned by same company.

ADDRESS: Avenida Imperio de los Inca Machu
Picchu Village
www.grupointi.com/restaurante
reservas@grupointi.com
TEL: +51 84 234312 or +51 84 242037

Above: You will meet Peruvians from across the country at
Machu Picchu, like these three young women from the
western edge of Lake Titicaca.
Center: Backpacks made from golons are typical of the variety
of goods available at the market.
Below: The Waman Hotel and restaurant.

PARACAS PENINSULA: PARACAS, PISCO, ICA, NAZCA

Driving south from Lima on the Pan-American Highway, along the Pacific coast for 4 hours brings you to the Paracas Peninsula. Famous for large necropoli, or burial grounds, discovered in 1925, this is the source of the fabulously embroidered textiles you'll see in museums. Between 2,000 and 2,600 years ago, the Paracas culture flourished on the south Pacific coast in what is now Peru. Paracas gravesites excavated by Peruvian archaeologist Julio Tello contained over 400 bodies. Individuals were buried alone or in multiples in the hot, dry desert sand, and wrapped in dozens of large, elaborately decorated textiles, some as long as 100 feet. People of the Nazca culture, living about 50 miles (80 km) south, also wrapped their deceased in amazing woven or cross-looped funerary textiles. The mummy bundles were often as tall as 5 feet and as wide as 7 feet. The desert environment was perfect for mummification of the bodies, and the dry, dark underground chambers preserved the textiles' fibers and colors. From the quality of the wrappings and grave offerings such as gold jewelry found buried with the bundles, archaeologists concluded that many of the individuals were elite, and had purposeful cranial deformations.

Political conditions in Peru in the 1930s led to mass looting of many of these tombs before archaeologists could properly excavate them. Around 1931, a hundred of the finest (looted) textiles were illegally sent to Sweden by the Swedish ambassador to Peru. In 2014, Sweden finally began the repatriation process from the Gothenburg Museum where the precious pieces had been on display. One of the most stunning and labor-intensive pieces, a mantle or shoulder covering made entirely of complex crossed-looped figures, was first to be returned to Peru.

The Paracas and Nazca pieces that Julio Tello was able to rescue were protected and archived in Lima at the National Museum of Archaeology. The Amano Textile Museum in Lima has other splendid examples, as does the Julio Tello Site Museum (see page 70). The Brooklyn Museum in New York City displays an incredible Paracas mantle example with ninety little figures around the edges; they also maintain a good collection of ancient, looped four-pointed caps from Peru.

Within the region of Ica, the most popular stop is Paracas, as it can be reached by bus from Lima in 4 hours. Paracas National Reserve boasts pristine, sprawling beaches and rocky islands teeming with marine birds and colonies of sea lions, fur seals, and Humboldt penguins.

Getting to the Paracas Peninsula

Lima to Pisco by car or bus is about 4 hours, 143 miles (89 km) via the Pan-American Highway.
Paracas is another 10 miles (6 km) south of Pisco.
Lima to Paracas: 4 hours, 152 miles (245 km).
Lima to Ica: 4.5 hours, 191 miles (307 km).
Lima to Nazca: 273 miles (439 km).
From Nazca you can stop and fly over the famous Nazca Lines or continue the bus trip to Arequipa, Puno, and onward to Cusco. This southern route is mostly flat terrain and safer than the trans-Andean roads.

NAZCA LINES

Iconic motifs such as hummingbirds and monkeys from the famous and enigmatic Nazca Lines adorn textiles and jewelry made throughout of Peru. These "lines" are enormous geoglyphs or symbols and figures scraped into the rocky surface of the hills near the town of Nazca. They're so large that you can discern the entire shapes only from the air. The glyphs depict creatures, geometric lines, and spirals, some 300 in all. One of the largest is a bird 990 feet long (300 m). From archaeological remains it was determined that they were made by the pre-Inca Nazca culture. Their meaning and function are still debated. I highly recommend taking a flight over the lines.

Section of tiny cross-looped hummingbirds and flowers from a Paracas textile fragment; dyed alpaca. Typically the eight groups of tail feathers would have been attached to the edge of a mantle, making a fringe of little birds around the piece.

Owned by American Jonathan Green, the **Nazca Flights** company offers several exciting and safe flights in Cessna 206 airplanes over the coastal hills to fully appreciate the enormous hummingbird, spiral, whale, and spider, among many others, formed on the desert's surface.

ADDRESS: Avenida Perotti, Ica
www.nazcaflights.com
info@nazcaflights.com
TEL: +51 975612550

Museums

REGIONAL MUSEUM OF ICA/*Museo Regional Adolfo Bermúdez Jenkins*
While you are in Ica, visit the Regional Museum that contains treasures from the Nazca and Paracas cultures. The desert inhabitants of the Paracas/Ica area buried their dead in the dry sands, thus preserving the mummies and the textiles wrapped around them; braided hair styles are still visible on several heads. The museum is small but has exquisite embroidered textiles and ceramics and some interesting mummies with purposely deformed skulls.

ADDRESS: Avenida Ayabaca 8th block, San Isidro, Ica (a block from the plaza)

TEL: +51 34234383
HOURS: Tuesday–Sunday, 8 a.m.– 7 p.m; closed Monday

JULIO C. TELLO SITE MUSEUM/ *Museo de Sitio Julio C. Tello*
Known as the father of Peruvian archaeology, Dr. Tello excavated the first funerary bundles from the Paracas necropolis in 1925. The 2,000-year-old mummies were enveloped in yards and yards of cotton cloth embroidered with dyed alpaca fiber designs that stunned the world with their sophistication and subtlety. Over 400 mummy bundles were eventually found by Tello in the 1920s at Cerro Colorado, near the present-day museum site. The old museum was destroyed by earthquake and the new modern one opened in 2016; it's not large but has some valuable textile examples. Much of Tello's collected textiles now reside in the National Archaeology Museum (*Museo Nacional de Arqueología, Antropología e Historia del Perú*) in Lima.

LOCATION: Reserva Natural de Paracas, Puerto San Martín (about 13 miles [21 km] from Pisco)
museojuliotello@cultura.gob.pe
HOURS: Tuesday–Sunday, 9 a.m.–5 p.m.; closed Mondays

Embroidered fragment of a band from the Paracas necropolis. Detailed mythical creatures such as these with headdresses clothing, and accessories were often depicted in these decorative stem-stitch bands and in miniature cross-looped figures.

AREQUIPA

The beautiful "white city" of Arequipa sits in the Chili River Valley, in southern Peru, about 600 miles (1,000 km) south of Lima along the Pan-American Highway. Driving from Lima by car takes about 14 hours. Although Arequipa is just 65 miles from the Pacific Ocean, three snow-capped and dormant volcanoes surround the city. The highest is Misti at an impressive 19,098 feet (5,821 m). The town itself is much lower than Cusco and Puno, at only 7,550 feet (2,300 m) above sea level, so inhabitants and travelers enjoy a temperate climate for much of the year.

Founded in 1540, Arequipa's colonial builders used white volcanic rock to construct the lovely buildings and churches around the central plaza. The beautiful historic center was declared a UNESCO World Heritage site in 2000. Due to several large-scale irrigation projects, agriculture in the valley has prospered and the area has become a major processing center for alpaca and llama fiber and sheep's wool. The famous Michell alpaca yarn company is based here.

A herd of Michell alpacas grazes outside of Arequipa.

Wititi dancers in intricately machine-embroidered outfits take a break from the festivities. Performed only in the Arequipa region, this traditional dance has seen a resurgence since it was declared a UNESCO Cultural Heritage.

Getting to Arequipa

From Lima: There are daily flights from the Jorge Chavez airport in Lima to the airport in Arequipa: 1-hour flights with LATAM Airlines, Avianca, or LC Peru.

Cruz del Sur, Tepsa, and Oltursa buses go down the coast from Lima, often at night, which is fine because it isn't a particularly beautiful route. Peru Hop takes several days and you get to stop and see interesting things along the way in daylight. Straight through this route takes 15 to 17 hours with costs ranging from US$25 to $50, depending on the kind of seat/recliner service that you request for the three nonstop companies listed.

From Cusco: It takes less than an hour to fly over the Andes from the Velasco Astete airport in Cusco to the Arequipa airport.

By bus, the trip from Cusco to Arequipa through Puno takes about 12 hours. The usual companies offer this service; Cruz del Sur unfortunately only travels at night is on this beautiful route; cost is around US$33 to $45.

From Puno: This is an easy bus ride as it takes only 6 hours and costs US$23 to $30 or less, depending on the service and the company you use. There are three departures on Cruz del Sur, two in daylight.

Theoretically you could fly from Juliaca Airport, but all the flights now make 1 or 2 stops (Cusco and/or Lima) and most take 6 to 8 hours, more than the bus. And you still have to get from Puno to Juliaca, which takes about an hour.

Museums

MUSEO SANTUARIOS ANDINOS

This is a small but fascinating museum dedicated to a sacrificed Inca girl named "Juanita, the Ice Maiden" upon her 1995 discovery atop Mount Ampato, near Arequipa. Juanita was discovered wrapped in a woven mantle, a head cloth, and a lliqlla around her shoulders. Museum displays show the many artifacts buried with her and shards of the textiles that enveloped her, as well as her 600-year-old frozen body. A video shows history of the discovery in the context of Inca society and beliefs.

> **ADDRESS:** Calle La Merced 110, Arequipa (a short walk from the main plaza)
> www.ucsm.edu.pe/museo-santuarios-andinos/
> **TEL:** +51 54 215013
> **ADMISSION:** 20 soles
> **HOURS:** Monday–Saturday, 9 a.m.–6 p.m.; Sunday, 9 a.m.–3 p.m.

ARCHAEOLOGY MUSEUM OF THE UNIVERSITY OF SANTA MARIA/Museo Arqueología de la Universidad Católica de Santa Maria

Only a few blocks from the Plaza de Armas, this good museum contains textiles, mummy bundles, ceramics, and grave goods from all the main pre-Hispanic cultures. University students and professors excavated many of the objects displayed here, authorized through the only university Archeological Studies program outside of Lima. The Museum focuses on objects from the Arequipa area. Admission is free.

> **ADDRESS:** Calle Cruz Verde 303, Cercado, Arequipa
> www.ucsm.edu.pe/museo-de-arqueologia
> **TEL:** +51 54 221083
> **HOURS:** Monday–Friday, 8 a.m.–5 p.m.

Shopping

Arequipa provides many opportunities to purchase textiles, especially those made with alpaca and vicuña. You will find many artisan stalls around the streets near the Santa Catalina Monastery. Calle Santa Catalina and Calle Pasaje Cathedral are two little lanes that have large shopping complexes. Along Calle San Francisco are more artisan shops to check out. Next to the Plaza de San Francisco in the old town jail is the local artisan market; this a good place to buy alpaca products and other handicrafts, and a great selection of leather goods as well, including bags.

FUNDO EL FIERRO

The city's primary craft market is located near the San Francisco Church. It is not huge but there is a good choice of handicrafts, including alpaca items, at the dozen or so stalls. A special artisanal fair with additional stalls is held throughout the month of August.

> **ADDRESS:** Calle Puente Grau 213, Arequipa

PATIO DEL EKEKO

This is a small four-story mall a couple of blocks off the Plaza de Armas. It's filled with many interesting little shops and is a great place to buy alpaca wool items, jewelry, textiles, and other locally-made products. It's near the Mercaderes bus station, which is a stone's throw around the corner from the Plaza de Armas. You'll find a few places to get lunch here as well.

> **ADDRESS:** Mercaderes 141, Arequipa
> www.patiodelekeko.com

INCALPACA KUNA FACTORY OUTLET

Located within the Patio del Ekeko, this is an outlet for Kuna luxury alpaca goods that includes a small alpaca/llama petting zoo.

ADDRESS: Calle Mercaderes 141, Int. A-1, Arequipa
www.incalpaca.com
TEL: +51 054 225550

A couple of blocks north you can visit Kuna's second store, Kuna Casona Santa Catalina.

ADDRESS: Calle Santa Catalina 210 Int. Local 1-2, Arequipa
TEL: +51 054 282485

MICHELL MUNDO ALPACA/Alpaca World

Set in beautiful grounds with lawns and fountains, the Michell alpaca center has alpacas and llamas to hug. There might even be some new babies. Fiber processing is explained—how they sort the fiber, clean it, and so forth. There are weavers from the Awana Kancha project in Cusco (that Michell helps support) at work with their backstrap looms. Textile Machine Museum shows the antique machines used to card and treat the alpaca. There is also an exhibition of the paintings, textiles, and artwork from their annual competition, and a shop selling the lovely alpaca products of the Michell brand Sol Alpaca. And when you have taken the complete tour and finished shopping, have a coffee or cold drink at the café.

ADDRESS: Juan de la Torre 101, San Lazaro, Arequipa
www.mundoalpaca.com.pe/
mundoalpaca@michell.com.pe
TEL: +51 54 202525, Ext. 115
HOURS: Monday–Friday, 8:30 a.m.–6:30 p.m.;
Saturday, 9 a.m.–6:30 p.m.;
Sunday, 9 a.m.–5:30 p.m.

Hotels

MIRADOR DEL MONASTERIO

A lovely hotel with nineteen rooms, in the historical center. It has comfortable beds, fabulous views from rooftop terrace, and is located across from the Santa Catalina Monastery. Pleasant common patio areas; breakfast included. Book on the website.

ADDRESS: Calle Zela 301 Cercado, Arequipa
www.miradordelmonasterio.pe/
reservas@miradordelmonasterio.pe
TEL: +51 054-225 122 or +51 054-224 923

A few hours north of Arequipa on the way to Colca Canyon/Cañón del Colca, are two lovely lodges:

TRADICION COLCA

This hotel has an observatory, a swimming pool, horseback riding, spa, restaurant with grill, hiking, and yes, you can also sleep in the comfortable rooms. Breakfast included. They organize tours and hikes around the area. Book online for discounts.

ADDRESS: Carretera Principal, Pueblo de Yanque, Chivay (next to the Instituto Agropecuario, the Fish Institute)
www.tradicioncolca.com
reservas@tradicioncolca.com
TEL: +51 959013543

COLCA LODGE AND HOT SPRINGS

Located at an altitude of 10,660 feet (3,250 m) and a few hours from the city of Arequipa, this lush hotel is built on the banks of the Colca River and is surrounded by hundreds of pre-Inca agricultural terraces that have been declared a Peruvian National Heritage.

ADDRESS: Fundo Puye, Yanque, Caylloma
Valle del Colca, Arequipa
www.colca-lodge.com/en/hotel

info@colca-lodge.com (reservations)
recepcion@colca-lodge.com
TEL: +51 54282177
WHATSAPP: +51 959994739

Restaurants in Arequipa

HATUNPA RESTAURANT

Centrally located, popular with tourists and locals alike, Hatunpa features seven types of native potatoes served with mouth-watering sauces and toppings. Vegetarian and vegan dishes are also available along with yummy desserts and a long list of craft beers. Friendly service; good for lunch or dinner.

> **ADDRESS:** Calle Ugarte 208, Arequipa
> **TEL:** +51 54 212918

EL TÍO DARÍO

Favored as a spot for a relaxed lunch in a lovely flowery garden a couple of blocks away from the bustle of the city center. El Tío Darío (Uncle Dario) specializes in grilled and baked seafood and fish such as trout and sole, as well as ceviches and causas. There are several set lunch menus as well as à la carte choices, including great desserts.

> **ADDRESS:** Callejón del Cabildo 100, Yanahuara, Arequipa
> www.tiodario.com/restaurante#en
> Facebook: El Tio Dario
> **TEL:** +51 54 270473
> **HOURS:** Daily, 11 a.m.–4 p.m.

ZIGZAG RESTAURANT

Traditional Peruvian food with specialties of Arequipa, including vegan and vegetarian options. Meats served on sizzling volcanic rock platters. Recommended set lunch menu; friendly staff.

> **ADDRESS:** Calle Zela 210, Cercado, Arequipa
> www.zigzagrestaurant.com/restaurant#en
> **TEL:** +51 54 206020
> **HOURS:** Daily, noon–11 p.m.

TANTA

The open courtyard of a seventeenth-century mansion near the Plaza de Armas features the casual café called Tanta. The menu highlights innovative regional cuisine and local ingredients. Tanta adjoins the more upscale Chicha restaurant.

> **ADDRESS:** Santa Catalina 210 Cercado, Arequipa
> www.chicha.com.pe/en/arequipa
> reservacionesarequipa@chicha.com.pe
> **TEL:** +51 54 287360
> **HOURS:** Monday–Saturday, noon–11 p.m.;
> Sunday, noon–8 p.m.

Soft alpaca machine-knitted muffler by Michell Alpaca's Sol brand.

LAKE TITICACA

The big lake with the funny name has some impressive statistics: it is the world's highest navigable body of water and has a maximum depth of 922 feet (281 m). No less than twenty-seven rivers and streams flow into it. Located at the northern end of the altiplano on the border of Peru and Bolivia, the lake is so huge (about 120 miles by 50 miles) that it affects the ecosystem of the whole region. The freezing waters and reedy shores are home to rare birds and the endangered Titicaca giant frog. One legend claims that the original couple who were to lead the Inca people rose up out of the lake. For textile seekers, the lake holds two islands famous for knitting and weaving: Taquile and Amantani. I recommend visiting one or the other if you can.

The altiplano, or high plateau, stretches from northwest of Lake Titicaca in southern Peru to about 600 miles (965 km) to the southwestern point of Bolivia, dipping into Argentina and Chile. It is the largest mountain plateau after Tibet. Several major cities find their home in the altiplano, including Arequipa and Puno in Peru, and La Paz and Oruro in Bolivia.

PUNO

The town of Puno sits at the edge of Lake Titicaca at around 12,550 feet (3,825 m). Naturally, a high and cold place would be an important center of knitting, both for the locals to keep warm and for the traveler/craft market.

The town itself doesn't have a lot to offer in the way of other textiles or interesting sights, but there are a couple of good restaurants and several upscale lakeside hotels, so you can spend a pleasant night here on your way to somewhere else. It will be cold at this altitude, however; wear heavy jackets and choose a hotel with heaters. Puno is the jumping-off point for trips to Bolivia, Arequipa, or Cusco, and it is also the port for boats headed out across the lake to Taquile and Amantani Islands, 4 hours away ($6 each way).

The artisan markets here usually have a good selection of handknitted sweaters and gloves, detailed knitted dolls, and the ingenious little finger puppets found all over Peru and Bolivia. Occasionally, you might find typical caps from the nearby islands of Amantani and Taquile. For all manner of knitted goods, try the **Mercado Artesaneas** down by the railroad tracks on the route to the port and also the newer craft market set up all along the road to the docks.

Getting to Puno

Many travelers arrive in Puno by train or on buses run by reputable companies like Cruz del Sur and Peru Hop, arriving throughout the day from Cusco, Arequipa, La Paz, and other cities. Puno has no airport; the nearest is 28 miles (45 km) north of Puno in the unclean and unsafe city of Juliaca. Arrival there could be okay if you arrive in daylight and have a plan to leave soon. Avianca offers two daily nonstop flights from Lima to Juliaca Airport. Regular flights run from Lima to Juliaca (1 hour 40 minutes, direct) and back, and then you can take a taxi or trufi to Puno.

Hotels
FLOATING HOTEL IN PUNO
Currently closed for renovations but slated to reopen in September 2018, the Yaviri Hotel is a 150-year-old British gunboat fitted out with modern berths. If you saw the movie *Fitzcarraldo*, you'll remember this ship that was hauled over the Andes in kit form on mule-back. The restored ship floats at the edge of Lake Titicaca in Puno Bay, and you can spend the night on it. Email for reservations or check the website to see if it's open for guests; if not, Puno has plenty of other hotels.

www.yavari.org/en/history
reservasyavari@gmail.com

PUNO PLAZA HOTEL BY TIERRA VIVA
A good Puno choice on land is the Puno Plaza Hotel by Tierra Viva, an excellent Peruvian-owned hotel chain.

ADDRESS: Grau Street 270, Puno
tierravivahoteles.com/tierra-viva-puno-plaza
info@tierravivahoteles.com
TEL: +51 51 368005

Getting to Taquile and Amantani Islands

In Puno, there are numerous travel agencies that offer tours to the islands and access to homestays; I recommend Coyla Adventures. Many tours will include the **Uros Islands** which are interesting for a brief visit, to see how people really live on bouncy, thick mats of reeds anchored to the bottom of the lake. Men explain how the reed boats are skillfully wrapped and tied, some with capped, air-filled water bottles hidden inside for buoyancy. The women make chain-stitched embroidered hangings and pillows, not traditional in any way, but decorative. The women use the hard sell to convince you to buy; when you have had enough, ask nicely to leave or if you are at the dock, ask for a boat heading directly to Taquile or Amantani Islands.

Favorite Travel Agency in Puno

Coyla Adventures offers tours to Taquile and Amantani Islands and local villages. Owned by Rene Coyla and his wife, Irma, this ecological adventure company specializes in private or small-group day tours, and overnight or multiple-day trips. They have sturdy, covered boats and they employ terrific local English-speaking guides who will give you details about the local customs, nature, and ecology along your route. Rene was

raised on the Uros floating island called Santa Maria Jacinto, and Irma is from Puno, so they couldn't be more connected to the fascinating Lake Titicaca community experience.

ADDRESS: Calle Arequipa 608, Puno
www.uros-titicaca.com/
titicaca_guide@yahoo.es
CELL AND WHATSAPP: +51 998867112 or +51 989733723
Facebook: Coyla Adventures

You can also walk down to the boat landing and find a launch (*lancha*) there; many head out daily around 7 a.m. for the 4-hour ride. Boats should have life jackets and protective windows with a roof overhead. Dress warmly in windproof clothing; it is windy and very cold on the lake in the morning and evening.

TAQUILE ISLAND

The island lies about 28 miles (45 km) offshore from the city of Puno, on the Peruvian side of Lake Titicaca. Boats from the port of Puno motor over in about 4 hours. If you decide to visit an island, plan to spend the night (see page 80 for what to bring). The boat trip is too long to really see the island and return to Puno by daylight. Both Taquile and Amantani have active homestay programs; the very organized community leaders parcel out the visitors so that hospitality income is spread equally. It's really awe-inspiring to be on a tranquil island in the middle of an enormous lake and look up at the dazzling stars.

A knitter making a nontraditional brown, gray and white *chullo* for sale to tourists. Note how he drapes the yarn around his neck; this technique keeps the working yarn in place as he knits and helps to maintain even tension.

No roads or cars are needed on this hilly little island, only about 3½ miles long (5.6 km). It's crisscrossed with paths between houses, down to the port, and to the terraced corn and quinoa fields. Sheep, cattle, and llamas roam, kept from the crops by neat stone walls bordering the fields. About 2,500 people live on Taquile where they grow corn and quinoa and create textiles so fine and beautiful that in 2005, UNESCO declared "Taquile and Its Textile Art" as "Masterpieces of the Oral and Intangible Heritage of Humanity."

Even before the island was so recognized, the knitting men of Taquile Island had become well known in the Andean textile world for their skill at making fine chullos. Both because of and in spite of the travelers who visit their island home, the islanders still wear traditional clothing including finely woven belts (*chumpis*), chuspas, and tightly knitted chullos. Bachelors make their own chullos with a long, pure white top, and married men wear an all-red chullo. Rows of little motifs on red represent the *seis suyos* (six parts of the island) and other symbols stripe the lower sections of all men's chullos. Little girls wear a more pointy version of Papa's chullo with a ribbed ruffle to shade their eyes from the harsh high-altitude sun. The women are expert weavers and make patterned cotton belts and bags; some men also weave when they aren't planting quinoa or digging the potato crop.

Above: A priest blesses the weavers on Taquile Island.
Below: The community co-op on Taquile features dozens of chullos for sale in a variety of styles and colors, some traditional, some not.

On the main plaza at the top of the island, there is a two-story community store full of woven items and knitted caps. Many pieces here show the exquisitely fine patterns and smooth, even stitches that made the people famous for their textile work. Other items exhibit the changes that time and fame have wrought. The original men's chullos didn't have earflaps and were always red

Above: Faustino Quispe Cruz (right) and his son knit together in the family compound. Below: Women weave belts, bags, shawls, and blankets on pegged ground looms.

and white, but many caps for sale in the community store nowadays are turquoise blue or green and have the earflaps typical of the beanie shape favored by skiers and travelers. Indeed, the UNESCO website adds, "While tourism is regarded as an effective way of ensuring the continuity of the textile tradition, rising demand has led to significant changes in material, production and meaning."

Spending the night on Taquile, Amantani, or Uros

Things to take: Warm clothes, flashlight, water bottle, toilet paper, and any other items you absolutely must have for a possibly chilly night.

When you've climbed up the neat rock pathway from the boat docks to the main plaza, you're standing huffing and puffing at almost 13,000 feet (4,000 m). A community housing representative has probably already signed you up with a family for the night's stay. Around the small plaza are a few restaurants serving quinoa soup and fried trout; lunch and/or dinner may be included with your homestay fee. The rep will take you over to the family's rooms where you will be sleeping. When you arrive at the house, get the name of the homeowner in case you get lost, check during daylight where the bathroom is, and see if there is a flashlight in your room. If you see no lights (many homes now have solar panels) and you didn't bring a flashlight, ask for one. On Lake Titicaca, the night is very dark! There will be heavy, thick blankets on your bed—think x-ray protection, heavy.

You will love them in the middle of the night. Once you are oriented, walk around the island and meet a few knitters or weavers; have an Inca Kola on the plaza or visit the co-op store. Make sure you can find your house again; it can be helpful to take photos of your route as you go!

AMANTANI ISLAND

This island is north of Taquile and is larger, with about 4,500 inhabitants. I recommend staying here if you want a more authentic experience with fewer fellow travelers. There are some small pre-Inca stone sites that are interesting to explore. Islanders speak Quechua on both island settlements with few differences in culture or textiles. Here, as on Taquile, little girls wear knitted bonnets until puberty, when they don black head cloths. The Amantani bonnets have a knitted and gathered ruffle to protect eyes. Men knit chullos for their daughters. Celebrations on both islands are wonderful with everyone decked out in typical red and black clothing with handmade bags, belts, and knitted caps.

If you want to see the islanders on Taquile in full festival gear with caps, bags, and tassels galore, be there for Easter or the week after July 25, which is the festival of San Santiago (Saint James). There is a textile art fair around the same dates with loads of handicraft booths set up, but I have not attended it. For festivals such as the big Amantani Island festival in January or the Santiago festival in July, make arrangements ahead of time with Coyla Adventures or another agency.

Above: A woman spins while carrying her daughter who wears the traditional ruffled chullo.
Below: A Taquile weaver creates a long warp on her staked loom.

FESTIVALS and CELEBRATIONS

Somewhere in Peru and Bolivia every single day of the year there is a festival. Not content with the dozen or so rather staid events that some cultures celebrate, Peruvians (and Bolivians) find as many occasions (some say excuses!) as possible to have a joyous fiesta. The birth of a saint, the death of a saint, an earthquake that stopped, the death of Jesus, the resurrection of Jesus, the feast day of a saint, political holidays, birthdays, anniversaries, and hundreds of local variations make great reasons to dress up, dance, eat, and drink. Desirable components involve special clothing or fancy costumes, decorations, very loud music, dancing, fireworks, and processions through the streets.

Masked celebrants in Chinchero at the Festival of the Virgin of the Nativity.

It should be noted here that any quasi-Catholic event, specifically celebrating the Virgin of Candelaria (Candlemass) or Asunta (Assumption) or Carmen or whomever, indicates reverence for the same Virgin Mary.

People in rural farming communities engage in marginally Catholic festivities, but part of the ceremony always implores Pachamama (Mother Earth) for bountiful harvests, abundant rain, fertility for their llamas or for themselves, and so forth. They also perform rituals at sacred sites such as mountaintops that they call *apus*.

Listed here are some of the most interesting celebrations in Peru where you are most likely to see amazing textiles, costumes, and processions. Bolivians are just as enthusiastic about celebrations and share many of the same festivals, but they have their own special occasions, too (see pages 130-134).

3rd Thursday in January
Fiesta de la Santa Tierra/Sacred Earth Festival

Fiesta de la Santa Tierra is an indigenous event on Amantani Island. The main event is a race; the population divides into two groups that assemble at temples on the two peaks on the island. The temple of Pachamama sits on one mountain and on the other is the Temple of *Pachatata* or Father Earth. Runners dash from the peaks to meet in the middle amidst much revelry. Villagers wear traditional clothing for this colorful event. If you want to spend this night on the island, reserve a room far in advance.

February 2–7
Virgen de Candelaria, or *Carnaval*/Virgin of Candelmas, or Carnival

The Virgin of Candelaria's feast day is celebrated on specific dates, with equal fervor in Puno, Peru, and over the border in Copacabana, Bolivia, where the same figure is called the patroness of Bolivia, Our Lady of Copacabana. The event is the year's biggest festival in both towns and draws thousands of South Americans as well as international tourists. Over the years, the Puno event has become more and more like Oruro's Carnival (in Bolivia, see page 112), and has engendered heated competition and accusations of appropriation. Groups with dancers in fabulous costumes are the *Diablada* and the *Morenada*; some groups in Puno wear unique theme costumes that are not seen in Bolivia. February 2 is the main day, but some festivities and rituals continue for another few days.

An elaborate beaded chullo and mask on a dancer at the Paucartambo Virgen del Carmen or Mamacha Carmen festival.

Porters bearing the statue of Christ, resplendent in their finest traditional ponchos and chullos.

Carnival in Other Towns and Cities

Because Carnival relates to events on the Catholic calendar, the dates change each year. Generally, the main Carnival event takes place on a Saturday about 40 days before Easter and a week before Lent. You will need to check online for exact dates in specific places.

In Peruvian highland villages, local festivals at Carnival time are called *yunsada* or *yunza*; the people dance around a decorated tree that is ritually felled. If you happen upon such a rural ceremony, wait to be invited to participate or remain an observer (see Navigating Carnival on page 117). Cajamarca and Cusco both have Carnival dance groups that wear stunning costumes and dance tirelessly for hours at a time; in reality, most towns celebrate Carnival. And just when the townspeople have revived from Carnival, 8 days later processions of dancers and musicians celebrate the *octavo* around the Cusco Plaza de Armas and other main squares throughout Peru.

The Virgin of Candelaria or Candlemass in the south is celebrated especially in the towns of Cayma and Characato. The usual masses, processions carrying the Virgin and dancing with costumes take place. In Cayma, the Virgin is called Virgen de Cayma. Tall bamboo *castillos* or fireworks "castles" are constructed by local fireworks experts and set off in a whirling cascade of sparks at the end of the festival.

March or April, Monday before Easter, varies by year
Señor de los Temblores (Taitacha in Quechua)/Lord of the Earthquakes

One of my favorite events, the rather somber Lord of the Earthquakes procession happens only in Cusco, Peru, where a miracle took place. Legend says that in 1650, there were long, hard tremors that terrified the inhabitants. Prayers didn't work so they took a painting of Christ out of the church to pray in the Plaza de Armas. The earthquakes stopped. A large and beautiful statue of Christ was later sent to Cusco from Spain. It's unclear whether it arrived with black skin or (as some say) the smoke from the candles in the cathedral turned it black. In any case, on the Monday afternoon before Easter, the black Christ statue is in the cathedral, and each Easter Monday, it's taken out in a huge procession through the streets of Cusco, commemorating Christ halting the earthquakes. Forty-four strong men struggle to carry the heavy figure out of the cathedral and onto the street. It's an honor and a sacrifice to carry the statue, and the bearers must change off to another crew every half-block. Dignitaries and priests from local churches lead the parade, and school groups, brass bands, church singers, and religious brotherhoods follow the statue. (The event resembles the Inca custom of ritual processions of the mummies of their chieftains, high priests, and supreme rulers.) At least one group that carries the statue wears handwoven ponchos and beaded chullos, typical of the Ocongate region. They make deep melodic sounds by blowing big conch shells called *pututus*. To ensure good luck and blessings, spectators on the balconies toss handfuls of red flowers called ñucchu (*Salvia esplendes*) representing the blood of Christ falling onto the statue as it goes by. Christ wears an elegantly embroidered loincloth that is changed in each of the churches around the center of town.

In the morning before the procession, buy a bag of the red flowers and some traditional Easter cookies for a few soles in front of the San Pedro market, and you'll feel like a local! The best place to watch this spectacle (during lunch) is from one of the upstairs restaurants on the north or west side of the plaza (facing the cathedral, the streets to the left and directly opposite). The figure usually exits the church around 1 p.m. Look to see which restaurants have balconies overlooking the

A villager blows a *pututu* during the Lord of the Earthquakes procession.

street, and make restaurant reservations a day or two before Temblores. Then go upstairs and stake out a table near a balcony; that more or less gives you balcony rights for the event. The Plaza de Armas is crowded during the procession, but it is packed to capacity in the evening when the general blessing is given.

[The Spanish adopted the Inca tradition of parading mummies of previous Incas (kings) into their Corpus Christi rituals and ceremonies, taking fifteen saints and virgins on procession around the streets of Cusco. This is another example of Spaniards cleverly converting people because they "accepted" and incorporated indigenous sacred figures and traditions into their conversion efforts.]

March or April, varies by year
Semana Santa/Holy Week or Easter Week

The week begins on Palm Sunday (*Domingo de Ramos*) and ends on Easter (*Domingo de Pascua*). Holy Week in Peru is particularly spectacular in Lima and in the highland towns of Ayacucho and Tarma, where it is celebrated after weeks of preparation, with special foods and great passion. Images of various saints from churches of the area and fervent members of various religious brotherhoods (and sisterhoods) carry embroidered satin banners in Holy Week processions. In Ayacucho, Tarma, and other towns, artists, townspeople, and school kids make especially detailed, brightly colored "carpets," called *alfombras*, from flower heads and petals, leaves and branches. Processions (which will tromp right over the fabulous flower designs), Catholic masses, and indigenous dances are all part of the festivities. Women in the typical white hats and long skirts of Ayacucho dance to the music of brass bands. In the evenings, saints on palanquins decked out with light displays are transported around town, accompanied by religious song and loudspeaker blessings by the priest. In every town, vendors install booths in small plazas (or in Cusco, at San Pedro market) to sell special holiday foods and various crafts typical of the region. As for popular festivals everywhere, book hotels early for this event.

Women in traditional dress during a Semana Santa procession.

Late May to early June, varies by year
Señor de Choquekillka/Pentecost Festival

Señor de Choquekillka is the patron saint festival of Ollantaytambo, combining dances, food, and rituals of the region with observation of Pentecost, which marks the end of the Easter season in the Catholic Church. The festival is one of the most important in Ollantaytambo and lasts nonstop for four days.

This is a great place to see street dancers in stunning embroidered and sequined outfits with papier-mâché animal masks (similar to the ones in Paucartambo) and spectators in traditional clothing. Bamboo towers strung with fireworks called *castillos* (castles) provide spectacular displays, but stay well away from them when lit because they include little packets of gunpowder that fling sparks dramatically. Book hotels in the Sacred Valley well ahead of time because Ollantaytambo is a little village and hotels fill up fast for festival dates.

One week before Corpus Christi, varies by year
Señor de Qoyllur Rit'i/Lord of the Snow Star

The observance of the Snow Star or *Qoyllur Rit'i* pilgrimage involves a long hike to a remote site in the Ausangate mountain region. Qoyllur Rit'i constitutes an interesting demonstration of Spanish and Andean indigenous beliefs; the pilgrims venerate apus, or Andean mountain gods, but the event also involves crosses and marginally Catholic religious ceremonies. Pilgrims traditionally wear knitted face masks against the cold and walk for many hours, having to pass by nine crosses and shrines. Certain figures called *ukukus* traditionally wear shaggy woolen outfits from head to toe in addition to the masks; they have the special task of climbing higher to the glaciers to carry back blocks of ice with sacred or medicinal qualities. An image of the Lord is carried to his sanctuary at Sinakhara, at about 15,000 feet (4,600 m). I have not done this walk, but it has become very popular: recent photos show many travelers getting involved for the "energy," and enormous fields of orange and blue tents spread over the hills at the base of the walk.

Ukukus clad in shaggy woolen costumes hike the Ausangate mountains during the Lord of the Snow Star celebration.

June 16–24
Inti Raymi/Inca Rite of the Winter Solstice

Inti is the Quechua word for the sun; Inti Raymi is an ancient rite of the Incas honoring the winter solstice. The people of Cusco celebrate the week before the solstice with nightly parades and fireworks and music in the Plaza de Armas. From their houses, *Cusqueños,* in indigenous solidarity, hang the city's rainbow-striped flag representing the Inca Empire, known in Quechua as *Tahuantinsuyo*. The night before Inti Raymi, June 23rd, brings another huge celebration in the Plaza de Armas with street dancers in traditional costume.

On the day of June 24, thousands of Peruvians and international visitors celebrate Inti Raymi, with a procession from the *Koricancha* (Sun Temple) to a reenactment in an open field in the ruins of Sacsahuayman above the city. Bleachers set up for spectators form a U-shape and the drama takes place in the center. Performers spend months practicing and considerable amounts of money on their costumes. The event has become huge and very commercialized; seats are chosen and tickets bought online. Despite being so commercial, in the impressive open-air site of Sacsahuayman, it's still exciting to see the costumes and the drama. Make reservations well in advance of this holiday.

June, Sixty Days after Easter Sunday
Corpus Christi/Holy Eucharist

Held in June, on the ninth Thursday or 60 days after Easter Sunday, Corpus Christi coincides with harvest season on the Inca calendar when they held rituals and ceremonies to honor Inti, the Sun God, for their bounty. Corpus Christi has been celebrated in Peru since colonial times, but it's especially impressive in Cusco with the street decorations and processions of images of saints and virgins in glittering embroidered clothing wending their way through town to the plaza and the cathedral. You can view all the processions best from the balconies of establishments around the Plaza de Armas, but it is also possible to stand on the sidewalks if you can find a good spot. At night, crowds gather for a vigil that lasts until dawn. Typical foods are served such as *chiriuchu* (spicy guinea pig, chicken, sausage, corn), beer, *chicha*, and cornbread.

July 14
The Wititi Dance

This folkloric celebration takes place in the towns of Chivay and Yanque with groups of dancers and bands. The Wititi Dance of the Colca Valley is a traditional folk dance that in 2015 earned UNESCO's designation on its list of Intangible Cultural Heritage of Humanity. July 14 was declared the Day of the Wititi Dance, but you can also see it on other dates such as December 8 in the village of Chivay in the Colca Valley.

The dance portrays potential lovers during a courtship ritual. Both men and women wear layers of embellished skirts. Under highly decorated vests the women wear fancy blouses, and one layer of their thickly embroidered cotton or velveteen skirts is pinned up in front, to show off the next skirt. Their skirts exhibit the intricate applique and straight-stitch machine embroidery made famous by artisans of the whole area. Embroidery in horizontal rows with lace and trim borders the skirts. Men wear white dress shirts over their skirts, with rolled up textiles crisscrossed over their shoulders, and fringed hats. Women use a smaller decorated hat. The Wititi is danced in rows of male and female couples; part of the dance involves twirling in one direction and then the next, showing off their many decorated skirts.

According to UNESCO, "The dance coincides with the beginning of the agricultural production cycle and symbolizes the renewal of nature and society. The dance consolidates social ties and strengthens cultural identity with villages in the Colca Valley competing to produce the best ensembles, thereby continuously renewing the dance while maintaining its traditional character."

A young woman from the Colca Valley performs the Wititi dance in traditional costume.
Opposite: Celebrants of the Virgen del Carmen in Paucartambo wear elaborately embroidered costumes and masks.

July 16
Virgen del Carmen/Virgin of Carmen

The small highland town of Paucartambo is famous for the *Virgen del Carmen* festival, which takes place over four days, with the principal days from July 15th to 17th. The Virgin is known locally as *Mamacha Carmen*. The festival consists of traditional dances, with some dancers wearing embroidered costumes and papier-mâché masks.

August 15
Virgen de Ausunta/Virgin of the Assumption

The *Virgen de Asunta* is very big in both Qoya (or Coya) and Calca, which are small towns in the Sacred Valley near Pisac. The Virgin is carried in procession by dancers masked as devils; paper and bamboo altars are paraded around town and participants wear wonderfully elaborate costumes. Arequipa also celebrates the feast of the Virgin of the Assumption, and the anniversary of the city's founding, with a fair featuring nonlethal *peleas* (bullfights). A week of processions and parades draws international artists. There are the usual fireworks and parade with sports and cockfights. Different districts and towns compete for the best dancing.

September 7–9
Virgen de las Peñas/Virgin of the Rocks

This is a typical fiesta in Castilla and Aplao including a Catholoic mass, a lot of music, and a lot of fireworks. You'll see a great display of pious revelers on the 8th with the procession of the sacred virgin statue around the town. On the 9th, blessings and benedictions are offered. Festivities take place in and around the church of San Pedro de Aplao and the Plaza Buenos Aires. Traditional foods are shrimp, guinea pig, chicken and pork, and the local pisco or grape brandy.

October 10
Virgen del Rosario/Virgin of the Rosary

In the districts of Urcos (Province of Quispicanchis), as well as Combapata and Checacupe (south of Cusco), homage is paid to the patron saint of the town with processions, artisan booths, bullfights, and hearty *pachamancas*, which are traditional meals of meats and potato varieties cooked in shallow pits over hot stones.

November 5
Puno Week

Puno Week, celebrated during the first week of November, recognizes the town's founding and its designation as the Folkloric Capital of Peru. Festivities include a reenactment of the Inca origin legend that says a sacred couple rose from the holy waters of Lake Titicaca to found the Inca Empire. Dressed in elaborate costumes with golden headdress and scepter, Manco Capac and Mama Ocllo dramatically arrive on shore on large and fancy reed boats. Hundreds of players accompany them in a major procession that leads from the shores of the lake to the town stadium for official events. Street dancing, drinking, and loud music continue until the wee hours of the morning.

December 24
Santurantikuy/Buying the Saints

This Christmas market in Cusco has been a Christmas Eve tradition for over 500 years. Early in the morning on December 24th, hundreds of artisans come to Cusco from the surrounding area to set up on the Plaza de Armas and sell their ceramics, textiles, and other artisanal goods until the evening. Cusqueños visit the market to buy nativity figures and greens or moss to arrange in their home nativity scenes. The plaza is decorated with lights and it's very festive. The market is interesting to experience as a cultural event. The National Institute of Culture has declared Santurantikuy a National Cultural Heritage.

The iconic reed boats of Lake Titicaca and the Uros Islands.

December 25
Christmas

Christmas celebrations take place all over Peru; in some areas, Christmas Eve is more important than the 25th of December. In cities such as Lima, Christmas is similar to the holiday in the United States, whereas in remote areas with animist beliefs, it may not be celebrated at all. Treats called *chocolatadas* consisting of hot chocolate, cookies, and perhaps small presents are offered by churches, businesses, and wealthy or generous people to those in need, especially children, in the weeks leading to Christmas.

Children from the community of Chahuaytire in the Peruvian highlands celebrate Chocolatadas.

AMAZON

ANDES

*Cobija

Lake Titicaca
*Copacabana

*La Paz
*Achocalla

*Cochabamba

*Oruro

*Santa Cruz

*Aiquile

*Sucre

Yotala*

*Tarabuco

Potosi*

*Tarija

BOLIVIA

Bolivia, from the air on a Google Earth map, looks impossible. In one landlocked country, the terrain changes from the ivory sands and white salt flats of the Atacama Desert in the west to the browns and tans of the high-altitude west-central plains and valleys called the altiplano. Then there's a jagged strip of bright white, the snow-capped Andes mountains. At the top, to the left of the snowy strip is the jumping puma shape of the largest lake in the Americas, Titicaca—half of it lies over Bolivia's northern border with Peru. Then look farther east on the map, and the other two-thirds of the country is bright green Amazon jungle!

Alpacas graze in the rugged landscape of the Bolivian highlands.

Bolivia receives fewer tourists than most other South American countries, only about 25 percent of the number of tourist who travel to Peru. Even off-the-radar Paraguay attracts more tourists than Bolivia. This implies both positive and negative factors for textile fanatics. Because this book covers Peru and Bolivia, I'll give some comparisons for the main cities and the Andean, textile-producing areas.

Because Bolivia has more indigenous people than any country in the Americas, and they create incredible textiles and occasions to show them off, we're able to see their handknitted and handwoven masterpieces at many celebrations.

In Bolivia, these festivals seem less touristic and more authentic than many in Peru, partly because fewer foreigners show up. The festivals of Inti Raymi and Qoyllur Rit'i in Cusco were begun by the Inca people and now tourists flood in to share the happenings, perhaps diluting to some extent the depth of meaning and symbolism for the local people.

Prices for travel, food, and lodging in Bolivia remain less expensive than in Peru, but increase every year as better traveler facilities are envisioned and constructed. (Both countries also have very affordable and clean, simple places to eat and sleep.) Some hotels and restaurants now offer excellent lodging and gourmet food, but there are fewer top-notch places than in Peru. There are not as many Bolivian travel companies, which means "unknown" remote villages are not crowded. Also, Bolivia has fewer incidents of theft and crime than Peru.

Both countries have plenty of stark and rugged terrain. Bolivia has half as many paved roads as Peru, which makes getting around more difficult—or at least less comfortable. Transportation is less frequent and less convenient than in Peru, although this is improving, too.

And Bolivia still requires an annoying, expensive online visa, whereas you feel more welcomed to Peru with just a quick, free passport stamp. Both countries offer amazing experiences for the traveler. Nevertheless, my personal tally concludes that for intrepid travelers who have a penchant for textiles, costumes, and festivals but who don't like hordes of tourists, Bolivia wins out for its authentic experience. To see both countries as many people do, I recommend starting in Peru to get used to the altitude, language, foods, and so forth, and then tackle less-traveled Bolivia.

When to go to South America? This may depend on your vacation time or your retirement date, and, of course, what you want to see and do. I usually go to high-altitude Cusco, Peru, for the Easter festivities and to high-altitude Oruro, Bolivia, for Carnival; both events take place in February or March. These seasons are not the best in terms of weather because it's technically the rainy season, but there's no choice if seeing particular celebrations is your goal. Besides, it doesn't rain all the time or even every day. And if you are near civilization when it begins to rain unexpectedly, vendors whip out cheap plastic ponchos to sell. May through September are the driest months.

Typical vacation months of June, July, and August are dry and very cold in the Andes; combined with high altitude, this period can be miserable if you aren't prepared with the right gear. When planning a trip, it's best to check weather sites for the cities you want to visit and the months of your travel, and then pack accordingly.

The view of Lake Titicaca from the Hotel Rosario in Copacabana.

I'll start in the north of Bolivia and go south through La Paz, Oruro, Sucre, and Potosí, hitting the textile centers I know along the way. Avid textile fans will discover places to see and buy textiles described here, but always be on the lookout for an impromptu festival and event or exhibition. Things change frequently, and Bolivians celebrate more festivals than could possibly be listed. If you hear of a patron saint's fiesta or a Pachamama ceremony, ask questions and try to attend.

I cite very good hotels and restaurants in the mid to upper price range but you could also spend a fraction of those prices and do a different type of trip. If you speak Spanish, or even if you don't, take a decrepit bus or ride over the altiplano in the back of a truck with some sheep and local folks to a village where someone said the weavers make incredible things. You'll probably make friends along the way, even if the whole conversation is gesticulated; they may let you sleep in a spare room and come to the nephew's wedding the next day. Bolivia is a great place for this sort of experience. Be friendly and open-minded, follow your gut feeling, and have an amazing journey.

Overlooking the fascinating city of La Paz.

Planning Your Trip

Visas are required for Bolivia; they are expensive (around US$160) and good for multiple visits for 10 years. Check online for current visa requirements for your country. There is supposed to be a "Visa on Arrival" service at the borders and airport, but I would be nervous about counting on it; call the embassy or consulate to see what is currently available. Don't be too horrified that they want a copy of a recent bank statement with your visa application; just block out your account number. Any account with a minimum of $1000 will do. Apparently, this is a tit-for-tat deal; United States Immigration requires similar information for Bolivians wanting to visit the U.S. I like www. travisa.com for online visas and visa help.

> **FUN FACT:**
> Bolivia has the world's highest international airport, the world's highest navigable lake, and the longest gondola car urban transit system in the world.

Arriving in La Paz

Most people fly into the El Alto International Airport at a breathtaking 13,323 feet altitude; make a note that you have arrived at the highest international airport in the world. If you feel particularly faint after walking into the terminal, ask the nurses in a little room near baggage claim for a blast of oxygen; many people need it when they first arrive. (I recommend taking pills of Diamox/generic acetazolamide for a day or two before you arrive and for several days after to alleviate symptoms of altitude sickness; ask your doctor for a prescription.) Hotels will arrange a taxi pickup for you if you email in advance; there are also taxis waiting to go into town. Don't be alarmed when your transportation wends through chaotic street markets and trashy neighborhoods on the way down into the basin of La Paz; it's all part of El Alto, a messy market town that sprang up on the altiplano around the airport without urban planning or building codes. However, if your flight arrives in the dark, late at night or early in the morning, definitely schedule private transportation ahead of time with your hotel. All hotels will arrange this, and a driver will meet you with a sign bearing your name. It's best to travel from the airport to La Paz city; do not stop in El Alto because the city can be dangerous at night. Better yet, arrive on a flight that comes in during daylight hours; the view flying into La Paz is stunning.

You might arrive in La Paz at the Terminal de Buses; if you are on the bus, you probably know what to do next. Taxis wait out front. Be careful of your belongings here.

Getting to Bolivia from Cusco or Puno, Peru

Note that Bolivian time is one hour ahead of Peru. (7 a.m. in Peru is 8 a.m. in Bolivia.)

From Cusco, take Peru Hop or Inka Express to stop in Puno if you want to see Lake Titicaca and an island or two. The Inka Express website provides other bus company choices also.

Otherwise, there are through buses from Cusco to La Paz (see bus information on page138). From Copacabana south to La Paz takes 4 hours by good nonstop tourist buses such as TurisBus from the Hotel Rosario del Lago. Puno to Copacabana takes 5 hours (includes crossing the Straits of Tiquina in

a motorboat with your bus on a barge floating alongside). Immigration and Customs between the two countries looks casual because of the general confusion about figuring out what to do and where, and which small rustic building to enter next, but the officials take their jobs seriously. Officers on break or local hangers-on will point you to the right place. Nobody at either post takes the slightest interest in what you might have in your bags. The bus goes right to the Immigration post at the border (where you can change spare soles to bolivianos). When you get off the bus, you will be shepherded to Peruvian Departure to get your passport stamped out on the Peru side. Then either get back in the bus or walk the short way uphill to the Bolivian side where authorities will scrutinize your visa (or this would be the place to get the "Visa on Arrival"). They'll stamp your passport to enter Bolivia and you're done. Use Transzela or Huayruro direct bus companies that, for US$7 to $11, go through Immigration at Kasani, a much prettier route than the Desaguadero–Yunguyo road. (See bus information, page 138.)

A colorful handknitted chullo from Bolivia with playful motifs in each strip of patterning.

COPACABANA

Built on the slopes of Lake Titicaca, Copacabana is a pretty little town with a big cathedral where fervent Catholics come to pray at Bolivia's most revered pilgrimage site. The site is so strikingly beautiful, with a round quiet bay and narrow sandy beach that the Inca revered it long before the Spaniards built a chapel and dedicated it to the Virgin of Candelaria.

The deep blue lake waters are very cold, and there are paddleboats in the shallow parts and fishing boats out further. Copacabana is a resort for *Paceños* (folks from La Paz) who want to relax in a hotel with lake views and eat fresh trout. The excellent museum here, Museo de Ponchos, makes a good introduction to Bolivian textiles. Most travelers see the church and the museum, have trout for lunch, and continue on south to La Paz or north to Puno and Cusco.

If you feel like you haven't been getting enough exercise while sitting on buses, take a break and do the 30- to 45-minute walk up Cerro Calvario, the pointed hill that overlooks the town. There are fourteen Stations of the Cross along the way. Climb at sunset for dramatic lighting, but the 360-degree views over the lake are stunning anytime.

My favorite time to be in Copacabana is for the early February Virgin of Candelaria feast day (also celebrated in Puno, Peru, and other towns) because the festivities include the Blessing of the Cars. A priest comes out of the cathedral at a specific time to bless new or newly purchased vehicles waiting in a row in front of the church. Owners open the hood and the priest says a few words and shakes holy water over the engine; I never tire of watching this spectacle. Beware of your possessions during this festival; the pickpockets are very clever and for some reason more plentiful than in other places.

PONCHOS MUSEUM / *Museo de Ponchos*

This is a museum of traditional clothing begun by Dr. Walter Jordan (see page 103 for his La Paz venue), this one focusing on men's ponchos. Situated near the edge of Lake Titicaca, it exhibits an excellent variety of handweaving forms and techniques, with most of the labels in English.

Poncho examples on display originated in thirteen far-flung and very traditional regions of the Bolivian Andes, including Kallawaya (Charasani),

Aroma, Bolívar, Northern Potosí, Tarabuco, and Jalq'a. There is also a fair-trade shop where weavers sell their textiles.

ADDRESS: 42 Calle Baptista, Copacabana
www.museodelponcho.org/en
info@museodelponcho.org
TEL: +591 2 2243601
HOURS: Monday–Saturday, 10 a.m.– 5:30 p.m.; Sunday, 10:30 a.m.– 4 p.m. If no response, knock on the door; often someone is inside to let you in.

Favorite Hotel in Copacabana

HOTEL ROSARIO DEL LAGO (owned by the same family that owns Hotel Rosario in La Paz) Constantly upgraded and modernized, this eco-hotel sits near the edge of Lake Titicaca. Solar panels cover the roof, and every room has thermal windows that face the lake. Sunset views from your room or the outside terrace are gorgeous. Colorful textiles and Bolivian folk art decorate all the rooms and the pleasant common areas. The suite at the top is divine, with a large sitting room, lake views, two bathrooms, and two bedrooms; ask to reserve it if you are a group of several people. The staff is very friendly, and the convenient TurisBus goes directly to the sister Rosario Hotel in La Paz.

The breakfast buffet is bountiful, and the Terradentro Restaurant is excellent, serving pink lake trout and a good choice of international dishes.

ADDRESS: Avenida Costanera, corner of Rigoberto Paredes, Copacabana
www.hotelrosario.com/lago-titicaca/book-now
reservas@gruporosario.travel
TEL: +591 2 8622141 or +591 73086364
RESERVATIONS: +591 2 2776286 or WhatsApp +591 76254988
TURISBUS: experiences.turisbus@gruporosario.travel
FOR BUS AND TOUR INFORMATION: +591 2 2798786

Cars line up outside the cathedral in Copacabana, waiting their blessing by the priest during the Virgin of Candelaria festival.

Restaurants

All restaurants in Copacabana specialize in delicious *trucha* or pink lake trout; just walk from the Rosario uphill to the cathedral and see what looks good along the main street, Avenida 6 de Agosto. Many serve outdoors on patio tables. The beach also has a row of stalls serving grilled or fried fish with french fries.

LA PAZ

You first view of La Paz may be shocking; it is an enormous bowl full of little red brick houses climbing the curves on all sides with a strip of skyscrapers down the middle. And the spectacular mountain is reassuringly visible from everywhere in town on a clear day, the towering 21,122-foot (6,438 m) snow-capped Illimani. Located 42 miles (68 km) south of Lake Titicaca at almost 12,000 feet, La Paz is the highest (de facto) capital city in the world. Spanish conquistadors founded La Paz in 1548 at the Inca settlement of Laja, nearer Lake Titicaca. Eventually, the town was moved to the bowl eroded by the Choqueyapu River and became the site of numerous indigenous and patriot revolts. The last one led to the Spanish American Wars of Independence and Bolivia's freedom in 1821.

Cholitas walk through downtown La Paz wearing the typical undersized bowler hat and fringed shawl (see pages 107–108). Cholita is a diminutive of the Spanish word *chola*, a derogatory term for those of mixed race.

The population today is around 1 million; double that if the El Alto satellite city is included. La Paz has got to be one of the few places in the world where lower-income residents enjoy a great view from their houses clinging to the walls of the bowl in the highest parts of the city and the affluent live in the lowest, flattest parts of the city. The months of May through August bring a freezing, dry climate, and the slightly warmer months of November through March receive the most rain. This means that during Carnival season in the wetter, slightly warmer months of February or March, you can still be comfortable as long as you pack a rain jacket.

[**Mi Teleferico** I highly recommend that you take a ride at some point on the fabulous new aerial tramway built by a German company; there are Red, Green, Yellow, and Blue Lines crisscrossing La Paz now, with plans for more. A long, silent ride with spectacular views costs only 3 bolivianos (around 40 cents). Bolivia is way ahead of other countries on this one. **www.miteleferico.bo/**]

Favorite Museums

MUSEUM OF BOLIVIAN ANDEAN TEXTILES (MUTAB)/*Museo de Textiles Andinos Bolivianos*

This excellent private museum was started in 1999 by the late Walter Jordan, an engaging anthropology professor with a passion for ethnic clothing and accessories. It is a bit hard to find, but radio taxis will call in to headquarters and find the little Plaza Benito Juarez. There is a sign outside, and you need to ring the bell to be admitted to the tranquil garden and the white tile-roofed home that houses the museum. Inside, two floors of rooms display authentically dressed mannequins from the main textile-producing areas of the country. Displays include valuable cultural context, such as the section on the ceremonial aspects of textile culture. Walter's wife, Maria Elena, and his son now manage the museum; she will be happy to take you through on a Spanish-language tour. You can also call for a private tour appointment if the days and hours are not convenient. This is a valuable experience in La Paz, not to be missed.

The admission fee is minimal; donations and social media reviews are appreciated. If you go in a taxi, they will call for one to pick you up when the visit is finished. There is a fair-trade shop downstairs called Qhatu Mutab, which usually has very good woven pieces and small embroidered items for sale.

ADDRESS: Plaza Benito Juarez #488, between Guatemala and Cuba Streets, La Paz

A man sports his festival awayo handwoven with a three-color warp.

www.museodetextiles.org/en/home
info@museodetextiles.org
TEL: +591 2 2243601
HOURS: Monday–Saturday, 9:30 a.m.–noon; 3 p.m.–6:30 p.m.; closed Sunday

NATIONAL MUSEUM OF ETHNOGRAPHY AND FOLKLORE (MUSEF)/*Museo Nacional de Etnografía y Folklore*

Consisting of two buildings, one modern and airy and the other from the late 1700s, this venerable museum has kept up with the times with a good research library and public events like conferences, ethnic music concerts, and traditional folk dances. Specializing in demonstrating the diversity of Bolivian indigenous material culture, permanent exhibits at this excellent museum include an entire room of Carnival and festival masks, dramatically displayed on black walls with a spotlight on each one. Another room displays antique weavings, and you can open flat drawers below the framed weavings to examine more finely woven pieces. And much to my delight, the curators have organized a new permanent exhibition of dozens of knitted chullos.

ADDRESS: Calle Ingavi 916, corner of Jenaro Sanjines, La Paz
www.musef.org.bo
musef@musef.org.bo
TEL: +591 2 2408640
HOURS: Monday–Friday, 9 a.m.–12:30 p.m. and 3 p.m.–7 p.m.; Saturday, 9 a.m.–4:30 p.m.; Sunday, 9 a.m.–12:30 p.m.

Shopping

La Paz is the best place in Bolivia to find a huge selection of older traditional textiles and also newer designs in knitting and weaving (the Tarabuco market is probably second best). It's also the central sales point for textiles bought by middlemen/textile scouts from villagers in the mountains and valleys as far away as Charasani to the north and Potosí to the south. In many remote communities, weaving provides an income and the people sell older weavings when they need money and/or tire of the old style. Fine examples show up regularly and this means that you will have great choice, but remember that a traditional textile bought in La Paz was almost certainly made elsewhere in Bolivia. Only some vendors know where the pieces originated so learning the provenance may not be easy. I have bought some unusual and undocumented knitted caps and woven awayos here. If you aren't too concerned with the origins of pieces and want them for their unique beauty, La Paz is a great place to buy textiles. You'll also discover an enormous selection of contemporary handknitted and hand- or machine-woven alpaca and wool clothing such as sweaters, cowls, scarves, ponchos, and so forth.

SACARNAGA STREET

Textile stalls and shops line Sacarnaga Street from Calle Illampu all the way down to the San Francisco Church and the big boulevard called the Prado. Stacked on the sidewalks or crammed into stores along Sacarnaga Street, a variety of handwoven awayos and chuspas will tempt fiber fanatics. The cross street Linares has interesting shops in both directions off Sacarnaga. Persistent textile buyers may find a special piece in one of the many shops in this general area. If you are standing in front of the San Francisco Church at the foot of Sacarnaga Street, the first antiques and

A textile stall in Sacarnaga Street with a variety of goods for sale.

artifacts store to the left is called Artesania San Francisco, at Plaza San Francisco #498. They have a good selection of older weavings, crafts, and interesting ethnographic pieces.

ARTESANIA SORATA

This group of rural and peri-urban artisans, using Andean textile techniques and their own creativity, work to provide a higher standard of living for their families. The Sorata project was begun in 1978 by North American Diane Bellomy who has spent 40 years collaborating with Bolivian villagers and city dwellers to encourage women to value their textile heritage and to use their traditional skills to make products for today's world. Shopping at Artesania Sorata helps with important funding to support literacy and health programs for the artisans as well as art workshops for kids in state children's homes and a children's hearing program.

Artesania Sorata products are immediately recognizable for their soft hues of hand-dyed natural fibers and original design motifs. The colors are produced by natural dyes that the group has researched and experimented with to bring the hues of their ancestors into their creations. The store offers a selection of handknitted alpaca sweaters and accessories for everyone. The large appliquéd wall hangings and pillows with Andean scenes are unique, as are the charming dolls, bags, and purses made with traditional methods and materials.

It is possible to visit the workshop or even volunteer in various capacities with Diane's group of welcoming women. Artesania Sorata is often looking for designers and artists to develop stylish fashion and marketable craft projects. Email Diane at cnsorata@yahoo.com. They welcome wholesale orders, design ideas, and help with their website.

ADDRESS: Calle Sagarnaga 303, corner of Calle Linares, La Paz
www.artesaniasorata.com
info@artesaniasorata.com
TEL: +591 2 2454728

Top: Appliquéd wall hanging from Artesania Sorata.
Center: A finger puppet vendor in Sacarnaga Street.
Bottom: Handwoven cloth with brilliant bird and floral motifs for sale at a Sacarnaga Street stall.

AYNI BOLIVIA FAIR TRADE

The Ayni fair-trade shop offers charming handmade items, uniquely designed and carefully made by Bolivian artisans. Finely embroidered or knitted objects, handwoven textiles, ceramics, gourmet coffee, and chocolate make shopping for gifts worthwhile. The handknitted alpaca baby and children's sweater/ cap/mitten sets of fine, soft fibers are particularly appealing. Products are of excellent quality, with unusual designs. Wholesale orders accepted.

ADDRESS: Avenida Illampu 704, left of the Rosario Hotel, La Paz
www.aynibuliviacomshopnuestras-tiendas-en-lapaz/
TEL: +591 76217335
HOURS: Monday–Friday, 9 a.m.–8 p.m.; Saturday, 10 a.m.–1 p.m.

ASARBOLSEM/*Asociación Artesanal Boliviana Señor de Mayo*

This fair-trade project known by the long acronym was organized by the dynamic and friendly Antonia Rodriguez to encourage solidarity among single mothers and women in need in El Alto and La Paz. The organization has grown and now has a large shop in El Alto. Most of the group are knitters who make sweaters, mufflers, ponchos, socks, and mittens with alpaca yarns. Antonia likes to experiment with new shapes and styles. There are cowl, scarf, and sweater styles here that you won't find in La Paz, and part of the experience is meeting Antonia and the knitting ladies. If you are a knitter, bring extra needles or yarn that you don't need, and they will be thrilled.

A sampling of alpaca knit scarves from the members of **ASARBOLSEM.**

You could take the spectacular ride to El Alto on the Red Line of Mi Teleferico (very nice, clean tram station at the end) and then get a taxi to her place. If you are feeling adventurous, go on a Thursday or a Saturday and also poke around the *16 de Julio* (16th of July) market, the largest open-air general market in Bolivia with an interesting section of "antiques." They welcome wholesale orders, design ideas, and help with their website.

ADDRESS: Villa Juliana, Avenida Norte 250, in the neighborhood of Primero de Mayo, El Alto, La Paz
srdemayo@entelnet.bo
TEL: +591 2 2831061 (call first before visiting)

WORKSHOPS of COSTUME EMBROIDERERS and MASK MAKERS

Dozens of artisans specializing in festival gear and accoutrements live and work in La Paz and in El Alto, the sprawling satellite city by the airport. Once Carnival or a patron saint's fiesta ends, artisans knock back a few beers and begin work on the next event's designs. Big or small festivals take place year-round in one town or another. Some dance groups or dancers require new costumes and the latest masks every year, so artisans work constantly to keep up with demand. (It's interesting to note that used outfits are often handed down (sold or rented) to dancers or musicians from smaller towns.) Workshops (*talleres*) of the easiest-to-visit costume and mask makers line both sides of Calle Los Andes, above the Rosario Hotel.

If you're well acclimated, start at Plaza Eguino at the end of Calle Illampu and walk up the street, checking out the store windows for a clue to what is happening inside. Most of the people here are welcoming if you are friendly and greet them respectfully (don't just barge in). If they aren't too busy, they may let you see their work. *"Buenos dias"* and whoops of admiration will get you a long way. You might drop in on costume embroiderers stitching sequins on horizontal frames, shoemakers tapping nails into the soles of devil dancer shoes, or artisans soldering tin parts of festival noisemakers called *matracas.* Near the top there is a large flower market across from the cemetery, and continuing uphill past the cemetery, you'll find more artisans working on costumes and accessories.

Alasitas **(Miniatures) Fair** is a huge local traditional event, not well known to travelers, that takes place in a dedicated park starting on January 24 and continuing for about a month, usually during Carnival. A priest at San Francisco Church comes out and blesses the Alasitas miniatures to kick off the event on January 24. The UNESCO team declared the Alasitas Fair an "Intangible Cultural Heritage of Humanity" event. Booths are set up in the afternoon and evening to sell food such as crunchy hot churros and the purple corn drink called *api*. The only textiles

Ekeko, Aymara god of abundance and prosperity, covered with miniature items that his owner desires.

here are usually knitted gloves and ingenious tiny sweaters, clothes, and detailed little Carnival costumes for Barbie dolls—but the event is so interesting that it's worth mentioning. Vendors also sell all manner of handicrafts, much of them related to Ekeko, an "Aymara household god," as he is called. Most Ekeko figures are 5 or 6 inches tall and made of painted plaster. He wears a knitted chullo and a little felt hat and has an open mouth to receive the cigarettes that his followers will light and offer him. Ekeko is related to one's good luck and prosperity, so his owner must buy desired objects in miniature and tie them onto the statue. Thus if a person needs a sewing machine or a video camera, she will buy little versions and tie them onto Ekeko. Vendors sell an unimaginable assortment of other tiny things here, including building supplies, tools, mini cereal boxes, bags of rice and flour, and so forth. Shamans will bless the items over a ritual fire if you ask. If there are children at home who own dollhouses, you can thrill them with miniatures from Alasitas.

WHERE TO BUY *CHOLITA* CLOTHES

It's fascinating to stroll along Max Paredes Street and look at the shops full of elegant outfits worn by the local Aymara-speaking women, called *cholitas.* Everything a cholita could want, from simple cotton aprons and eyelet petticoats to fancy special occasion outfits, is sold here along with all the accessories. You'll see cholitas as vendors and shoppers in La Paz, sporting too-small bowler hats, very full gathered skirts with three folded horizontal tucks near the hem (*polleras*), shawls with long macramé fringe (*mantas*), and flats. Women dancing in some festival dance groups wear matching outfits like this, but it is also the special occasion outfit for wealthy cholitas.

To find Max Paredes Street, go up Calle Santa Cruz from Illampu Street and veer right onto Max Paredes at the little circle park. This whole area is a market, selling kitchen goods such as tin cookie cutters, clothes, shoes, and almost anything else you can think of. Soon you'll come to rows of shoe vendors along the sidewalk selling flats in the colors that are in fashion at that moment, sometimes shiny gray, or light blush pink, or patent black. Some have the fronts made of clear plastic so you can see your toes. Farther up, in the big stores, you'll see rows and rows of hanging polleras made of satin brocade in glowing colors with macramé-fringed shawls to match. Every manta has a different pattern tied into the long fringe by hand. The signature black, brown, or gray bowler hats are sold here or on Illampu Street and are held on with bobby pins, in case you wondered.

Favorite Hotels in La Paz
HOTEL ROSARIO LA PAZ
I have always stayed at the friendly and safe Hotel Rosario. Its rooms and restaurant have been upgraded annually, with commensurately higher prices, but it remains the most pleasant and convenient place in the traditional market

Cholitas dancing at Carnival in Oruro, Bolivia. Discriminated against for decades, cholitas are now standing up for their rights to an education and recognition as valuable citizens.

area of La Paz. I keep returning, drawn by the cozy rooms decorated with Bolivian folk art, the pretty interior patios, and the gourmet restaurant. The associated travel agency with a desk in the lobby can help you with tours to Tiawanaku and Copacabana. A bus shuttles hotel guests to Copacabana and the sister Hotel Rosario del Lago at Lake Titicaca; see page 101.

The upstairs **Terradentro Restaurant** at the Rosario Hotel is excellent, serving Bolivian dishes with an international flair, beautifully presented.

ADDRESS: 704 Avenida Illampu, La Paz
www.hotelrosario.com/la-paz
reservas@gruporosario.travel for reservations
TEL: +591 2 2451658 or +591 2 2776286

The higher-priced **La Casona Hotel Boutique** in a restored seventeenth-century historic building on the Prado, just around the corner from Sacarnaga Street, will please travelers who want to be closer to downtown. The restaurant here is highly recommended also.

ADDRESS: Avenida Mariscal Santa Cruz 938
(commonly called the Prado), La Paz
www.lacasonahotelboutique.com/elhotel
info@lacasonahotelboutique.com
restaurante@lacasonahotelboutique.com for
restaurant reservations
TEL: +591 2 2900505

Favorite Restaurants in La Paz

The restaurant scene in La Paz is hopping
nowadays with some excellent choices.

Gustu (the Quechua word for flavor) is now
considered the best restaurant in La Paz. It's
located in the upscale Calacoto suburb of La
Paz, which is about a thousand feet lower than
the center of town. Renowned Danish chef/
humanitarian Claus Meyer opened it in 2012.
Dishes feature unusual combinations of Andean
and Amazonian ingredients. Meyer and his Danish
partners have started numerous successful
cooking schools in El Alto to give job experience
and employment possibilities to disadvantaged
youth. I have not tried Gustu yet, but it has
rave reviews and I like their values of social
responsibility; it's on my list. Tasting menus at
Gustu are expensive relative to other restaurants
in La Paz, but very impressive, and they use all
Bolivian ingredients. There is an information-
packed website in Spanish and English.

ADDRESS: 300 Calle 10 at Costañera, Calacoto
www.gustu.bogrupo-gusturestaurant-gustu?lang=en
booking@gustu.bo
TEL: +591 2 2117491
PHONE HOURS: Tuesday–Saturday, 10:30 a.m.–
4:00 p.m.
HOURS: Monday–Saturday, noon–3 p.m. and
6:30 p.m.–11 p.m.

Another restaurant with great reviews is the vegan
Ali Pacha restaurant with its appealing clean-
lined rustic brick, stone, and wood decor. The
innovative food is so good that dedicated meat
eaters still rave about their meals. It was started
by a Gustu alumnus.

ADDRESS: Calle Colón 1306, corner of Potosí,
La Paz
www.alipacha.com/en/us/
info@alipacha.com
TEL: +591 2 2202366
HOURS: Monday–Saturday, noon–3 p.m.
and 7 p.m.–10 p.m.

The Italian-influenced **Pronto Dalicatessan** (not
a typo; they like Salvador Dali) on Pasaje Jauregui
is only open for dinner. Walk down the stairs by
the sign to enter the restaurant. I have had some
excellent meals here; it's small and cozy with
great service.

ADDRESS: 2248 Pasaje Jauregui (a little lane
called a "passage") between 20 de Octubre and
Fernando Guachalla streets
TEL: +591 72599983
HOURS: Monday–Saturday, 6:30 p.m.–11:00 p.m.

For good sandwiches, salads, and smoothies, the
Banais Cafe, has great coffee and is a relaxing
place to eat. It's located on Sacarnaga Street
below Murillo Street (opposite the side of the San
Francisco Church).

And if you want to ride the fabulous new and
inexpensive Mi Teleferico aerial tramway, take
the Yellow Line down to the end of the line in
Calacoto to the good **Alexander's Cafe** for a lunch
of large servings of American-style favorites. You'll
need to walk a few blocks to the restaurant or get
one of the taxis waiting at the station; they should
know where Alexander's is.

ORURO

Formerly a booming silver and tin mining town at a 12,000-foot altitude, Oruro suffered an economic recession in 1985 when the price of tin crashed worldwide. UNESCO recognized Oruro's Carnival for "Oral and Intangible Heritage" in 2001 and that gave a boost to the town. In Oruro, tourism related to Carnival is an important part of the economy, although mining continues on a small scale.

Spectacular knitted leggings with traditional diamond patterning are a common feature of men's Anata Andina costumes.

Festivals in Oruro

Members of an Anata Andina dance group adorn themselves with apples in tribute to Pachamama.

Oruro itself only comes alive at Carnival time; the town is the "Folklore Capital of Bolivia." But in the surrounding altiplano regions in villages such as Toledo, Sacaca, and Bolivar, the people wear remarkable traditional clothing for a variety of patron saints' festivals and animist ritual occasions. Two main events in the same week thrill audiences and comprise the festivities that are anticipated all year: Anata Andina or the indigenous folks' parade honoring Pachamama (Earth Mother) on Thursday, and Carnival related to the Christian observance of Lent on Saturday. Anata means "play and joy" in the Aymara language (in Quechua it's Pujllay). Andean villagers use the word for their age-old potato-planting fiestas, celebrated yearly during the February rainy season. Clever Catholic priests long ago succeeded in likening Virgin Mary to Pachamama and influencing the rural population to the extent that these primordial nature and harvest rituals now coincide with the feast day of the Virgin of Candelaria.

When speaking of Oruro Carnival events, Anata refers to the Thursday event where participants dance along the same 2½-mile (4 km) route that the Saturday Carnival will follow. Important community leaders perform an intriguing *Ch'alla,* or offering, to Pachamama at Avenida Civica, the widest part of the route with bleachers on both sides. They place coca leaves down on a small, square handwoven cloth called a *tari,* and add molded sugar plaques, candies, confetti, and flowers. With ceremonial incantations, they sprinkle the items with the strong, clear alcohol or chicha that always figures in an offering to Pachamama.

These two events, Anata and Carnival, involve diverse segments of Bolivian society and differ not only in the religiosity of the rituals and ceremonies but also in what the participants wear.

Anata Andina participants wear ornate and fancy new versions of their usual type of clothing, like North Americans might wear a tuxedo or a ball gown. The Carnival dancers who perform on Saturday put on elaborate costumes, like North

Above: Community leaders make an offering to Pachamama along the Anata Andina parade route.
Below: It's easy to distinguish the Anata Andina dress (left) and Carnival costumes (right).

Anata Andina celebrants embellish their traditional dress with vegetables in honor of Pachamama.

The Carnival parade route ends at the Cathedral.

Americans might wear at a masquerade ball or for Halloween. Anata Andina remains one of my favorite places to see new and intriguing textiles. The festival committee organizes Anata, inviting dozens of indigenous groups from the altiplano area around Oruro to participate on Thursday. Villagers wear handmade festival dress that is traditional to their specific region and ethnic community. Because Anata gives thanks to Pachamama and her bounty, green branches, red quinoa stalks, and other agricultural products adorn the dancers. One group dances with necklaces of green apples. Men play handmade wooden flutes and drums in the procession; decorated llamas and an occasional black and white cow accompany some groups. It seems like every year some Anata dancers layer on more belts, chullos, and awayos to show off their superb textile skills. The organizing committee awards humble and touching prizes such as wheelbarrows and shovels to the best dance group.

The Oruro Carnival is a religious pilgrimage with more joy than most; the exuberant dancers and musicians promise the Virgin of Socavón (Virgin of the Mineshaft, also Candelaria) that they will perform along the 2½-mile (4 km) route up to the Cathedral as a sacrifice in exchange for her blessing. Every year, folkloric dance groups from all over Bolivia converge in Oruro for the event. In 2018, fifty-four dance groups with numerous *bloques,* or troupes, participated and it was "guesstimated" that 28,000 dancers, 10,000 musicians, and 400,000 tourists jostled for space in the crowded streets. That hardly seems possible to me, but spread out over the whole town, maybe.

The Saturday Entrada is the grand entrance to Carnival. Participants from the most prestigious groups are urban dwellers who might be doctors, systems analysts, railroad workers, lawyers, university students, or teachers. These most impressive and wealthy groups dance in professionally designed costumes made of fabrics such as lamé and satin, luxuriously embellished with intricate patterns in sequins and beads. Groups such as the Diablada and Morenada wear costly metal or plaster masks. Students and older, less affluent dancers and musicians scrimp and save to have impressive costumes for the event. For everyone involved, it not only has social importance but participants are making a sacrifice or pilgrimage to obtain the blessing of the Virgin of the Mineshaft.

Carnival costume embroiderers, mask makers, and shoemakers work in *talleres* (workshops) all along **Avenida La Paz** in Oruro. Shoemakers create hundreds of matching custom-made shoes for dance groups—from *Diablesa* boots to platform heels for the *Caporales* dancers. Heavily embroidered and complex Morenada costumes and intricate plaster and glass *Diablo* (devil) and Lucifer (king of devils) masks count among the most interesting products of the workshops. Get a map of town and walk away from the main plaza, six to eight blocks down Avenida La Paz, or find a taxi and explain that you want to see the *mascareros*. If you ask nicely, most artisans will welcome you in to take a look around, provided you go a week or so before the big Saturday Carnival Entrada event because they are

slammed with last-minute orders. In the days leading up to Saturday's Entrada, artisans rush to finish masks and costumes; most won't have time to show you around, but you can still peek in the doors.

Because these festivals relate to Easter and Lent, dates change every year. Carnival is supposed to end 40 days before Easter, but since the main Entrada event has to be on a Saturday, timing is not exact. Search the internet to learn the year's exact Carnival dates.

Above: Dancers in the Anata Andina procession.
Center: A dancer from Charasani makes her way along the Carnival parade route.
Left: A Morenada dancer at Carnival in Oruro.

Above: Anata Andina traditional dress involves complex layers of handwoven awayos, belts, and ribbons.
Below: Elaborate embroidered Carnival costumes and masks of Morenada dancers.

Getting to Oruro

To get to Oruro for Carnival, take a comfortable 3-hour bus ride over the altiplano from the La Paz Terminal de Autobuses (there is no airport in Oruro). There are also buses to Oruro from Sucre and Potosí. (See page 139 for more bus information.) Be sure to have hotel reservations in advance because the town fills up. If you arrive on Wednesday and stay until Sunday morning, your experience will be most complete, but if you're short on time, go for the big Saturday parade starting about 8 a.m.

The travel agency below has the best selection of 2- or 3-day Carnival packages at different hotels and may have a 1-day Saturday Entrada quick trip also.

Ludora Travel Club

ADDRESS: 584-25 de Mayo Street, Cochabamba
www.boliviatravelsite.com
reservations@boliviatravelsite.com
customerservice@boliviatravelsite.com
TEL: +591 4 4582363
WHATSAPP: 68583553

Favorite Museum in Oruro

ORURO ANTHROPOLOGY MUSEUM/
Museo Antropológico Eduardo López Rivas
The museum has four major areas: Archaeology, Ethnomusicology, Ethnography, and Folklore. There are no textiles per se, but the museum does have some complete Carnival costumes worn in past decades and a good historical collection of Oruro Carnival masks that shows their design evolution over the years. The museum is definitely worth visiting if antique masks and costumes interest you, as you will see nothing like these during Carnival.

Dancers in the Carnival parade in Oruro.

ADDRESS: Avenida España (quite a ways out of town; it is best to ask a taxi to take you)
TEL: +591 2 5274020
HOURS: 10 a.m.–6 p.m. (Carnival week will affect open days; call first)

Shopping

ARAO BOLIVIAN HANDICRAFTS/
Asociación Rural de Artesanías Oruro
This is the only shop that I know in Oruro that sells quality handicrafts and clothing intended to appeal to tourists. Organized by ARAO, the Rural Association for Handicrafts, the program encourages villagers living in the Oruro area to use traditional techniques to create marketable items with the goal of improving their economic situations. A large group of artisans from 150 communities in the region sell their work here at fair-trade prices, offering a good variety of alpaca sweaters, ponchos, cowls, shawls, mufflers, and mittens. It is located on a corner near the main plaza.

Jackets, plumed hats, skirts, and bags—you can find it all at Oruro's Bolivar Market.

ADDRESS: Soria Galvarro Street, corner of Adolfo Mier Street, Oruro
artesaniasarao@yahoo.com
TEL: +591 2 5250331

BOLIVAR MARKET/*Mercado Bolivar*

The Bolivar Market carries the best indigenous festival merchandise items not found elsewhere in such glorious abundance and variety. Upstairs in the building, a dozen booths overflow with a wildly colorful assortment of clothing and accessories used for Anata Andina and village celebrations.

Outfits of expertly machine-embroidered jackets and skirts in Day-Glo colors hang on the walls next to handmade, white, felted wool hats. To get ready to perform, villagers decorate the hats with a profusion of finely woven hatbands, plastic bead dangles, feathers, mirrors, and sequins, all for sale here. Wide handwoven belts and sashes of bright synthetic fiber with pom-poms and bead decorations dangle from the ceilings, along with men's diamond-patterned knitted leggings called *polainas*.

Some stalls carry a few handknitted new acrylic chullos, varying in price from $5 to $40, depending on quality, and whether the vendor thinks you as a gringo (outsider, foreigner) really want it. I love all the bright colors, but many Westerners find them gaudy. There are also many food stalls on the same floor.

Getting to Mercado Bolivar

It's an easy walk from downtown Oruro. Head down Bolivar Street (in the opposite direction from the cathedral/main plaza) and cross Avenida 6 de Agosto and the railroad tracks. Along this route, many vendors will be set up on either side of the street; the area is not dangerous, but be careful with your bag as in any crowded area. Continue on Bolivar Street along this outdoor market for three full blocks and soon you will see the big two-story market building to your left, with an entrance on the corner. If you don't see it, ask a street vendor, "Mercado Bolivar?" and someone will point you in that direction. It takes up much of the block and there are several entrances; the costume components are upstairs.

Favorite Hotels in Oruro

I usually stay at the aging **Gran Hotel Sucre** for its good (and reasonably quiet) location, one block off the main parade route. Rooms are clean, staff is helpful, and homemade breakfast is good (order scrambled/fried eggs, included). There is sporadic, free Wi-Fi in the lobby and in some rooms. Rooms vary greatly; ask for another if you don't like the one you are shown.

> **ADDRESS:** Calle Sucre 510, Oruro
> hotebol.com.bo/HotelSucre.html
> **TEL:** +591 2 5254110
> sucre@hotebol.com.bo

Flores Plaza Hotel is a more expensive, more modern hotel than the Gran Sucre, with a good breakfast and restaurant, conveniently located right on the plaza. It will definitely be noisy here during Carnival, but the bleacher seats are right out in front (that you pay for separately) and having your hotel room, restrooms, and food handy might make up for that. (See information on page 118 about sleep during Carnival.)

> **ADDRESS:** Adolfo Mier 735, Plaza Principal, Oruro
> www.floresplazahotel.com/
> plazahotelenoruro@yahoo.com
> **TEL:** +591 2 5252561
> **WHATSAPP:** +591 68350145

Favorite Restaurant in Oruro

The large and modern **Nayjama Restaurant** efficiently serves *Orureño* food, such as grilled lamb and Lake Titicaca trout. Enjoy the healthy cooked vegetable salad appetizer and tell them to hold the tasteless rice. The quinoa pie is great and the fresh fruit juices are delicious. Portions are enormous. You can share, then order the yummy homemade tropical fruit ice cream (perhaps *cherimoya* or *tumbo*) for dessert. Family-owned and friendly, the restaurant is popular with the Carnival crowd, when "special prices" (higher ones) are in effect.

> **ADDRESS:** Corner of Aldana and Pagador, #1880, Oruro
> **TEL:** +591 2 5277699

Navigating Carnival

Unless you go from La Paz to Oruro on an exhausting day tour, you absolutely must have previous hotel reservations for Carnival dates. In past years, a few modern hotels have been built in the center of town; check the usual sources for bookings but beware, some sit right on the parade route which means sleep will be difficult for 24 to 48 hours.

All hotels in Oruro charge elevated prices during Carnival, usually three or four times normal prices, and a 3-day package is usually mandatory (Friday, Saturday, Sunday nights). If you arrive for Anata on Thursday, you'll see many people selling bleacher seats as you walk around. Cheaper bleacher seats on narrow Calle Bolivar right behind the Gran Hotel Sucre and all the way up to the plaza are not great because the dancers can't spread out and people will be constantly walking in front of you. The best seats are on the three streets that border the main Plaza 10th of February, La Plata, Adolfo Mier, and Presidente Montes Streets, or farther up on the wide Avenida Civica where there is the most space for the dancers and musicians to perform.

Some hotel packages include box lunches and seats in the bleachers but if not, ask your hotel to help you find and buy seats, which can cost up to US$100 each. The Plaza Hotel and other establishments right on the main plaza bolt together bleachers and sell good seats out in front of the businesses; ask inside for cost and what is included (box lunch? restroom access?). Choose seats up a few rows or you'll have trouble seeing the action. Seats are numbered and during the daytime events, you will be expected to sit in your own seat but later at night when some people have gone home, you can move around. Food vendors line the side streets so eating is not a big problem, but take snacks and water because it's not easy to leave your seat once the parade starts. Old ladies sell cans of foam for spray-play, and kids sell cans of beer. A word to the wise: don't engage with drunk people at festivals.

Caporales dancers in their elaborately embroidered satin and sequin costumes.

The old adage "If you can't lick 'em, join 'em" applies to Carnival. You may decide the action is so enthralling that you sit in the bleachers long after bedtime, in time to see the Devil dancers shoot propane flames from their pipes into the dark, or set off the yellow, orange, and red smoke that forms a backdrop for dramatic photos of Lucifer prancing through it. You can walk up to the cathedral where it's okay to sit in somebody's abandoned seat to watch the tireless and electric dancing of the Caparoles until 3 or 4 a.m.; you won't be alone, and you'll have much better possibilities for great photographs. Late at night you can get right out in the middle of the street and shoot straight down at the parade; the flash will illuminate the front row of dancers in the streetlight and the rest of the

group will be darkened. The worst shots are taken perpendicular to the parade, with the audience behind the dancers.

If you need to sleep, here's how to snooze through the raucous, never-ending music. In anticipation of next year's Carnival (and international flights), I researched and bought little noise-cancelling earbuds, which work far better than earplugs. If you fly a lot, these little things are miraculous; they block out the engine noise of a plane while you watch a movie as well as the cacophony of brass instruments played by tired musicians. The very best earbuds tested were the Bose QuietComfort 20 or the wireless Bose QuietControl 30. You'll sail through the Carnival experience rested and happy, at any hotel.

SUCRE

A UNESCO designated World Heritage Site, the city of Sucre was founded by Spaniards in 1538 as *Ciudad de la Plata de la Nueva Toledo* (Silver Town of New Toledo) in south-central Bolivia on Charcas, the land of the local Yampara culture. In 1624, St. Francis Xavier University of Chuquisaca was founded by order of the Spanish king, Philip IV. It is the second-oldest university in the new world, and it maintains interesting museums of anthropology and colonial artifacts.

The city was renamed in honor of the leader of the fight for independence, Antonio Jose de Sucre, in 1839 when it was declared the first capital of Bolivia. Sucre, with its well-preserved white colonial buildings and tile roofs, remains the official or constitutional capital of the country and seat of the Supreme Court. La Paz, often presumed to be the capital, is the de facto capital. Sucre is a lovely city to relax in, and it has wonderful museums and easy access for visiting local villages. It's also the jumping-off point for trips to attend the Tarabuco market or *Pujllay* festival.

Local men in traditional dress shop on market day in Tarabuco, just outside of Sucre.

Getting to Sucre

At 9,214 feet (2,810 m) Sucre is almost 3,000 feet lower than La Paz. If you're traveling around Bolivia overland, Sucre's temperate climate and relatively low altitude will be welcomed. If you are just arriving in Bolivia from, say San Francisco, Boston, Buenos Aires, or Lima where you live near sea level, the best way to help prevent *soroche*, or high-altitude problems, is to fly into La Paz and connect directly to Sucre.

There are a couple of daily flights over the Andes from La Paz to Sucre's Alcantari Airport, situated 19 miles (31 km) south of the city. There are also many buses from Potosí and other main cities. See bus information on page 139.

Museums

MUSEUM OF INDIGENOUS ART/
Museo de Arte Indigena, or *ASUR*

Sucre's well-deserved claim to fame in the textile world is the comprehensive museum called ASUR, an acronym that comes from *Fundacion Antropologos del Sur Andina* or the "Foundation of Anthropologists of the Southern Andes," who founded the museum. ASUR is one of the best contemporary textile museums in South America, not to be missed. Videos at ASUR show festival celebrants playing musical instruments and wearing traditional costumes. An exhibition of unusual pre-Hispanic textiles gives valuable historical background to the contemporary work, and a weaver is always present in the shop to demonstrate her skill so you can watch her pick up threads to create patterns. The main collections display finely woven examples that show off the exceptional skill of female weavers from the three most important local weaving regions: Jalq'a, Tarabuco,

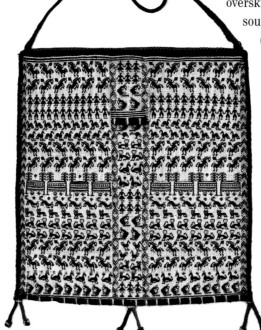

A chuspa, woven in black for mourning observance, features tiny figures of everyday life characteristic in the weaving of Tarabuco.

and Tinquipaya. The rectangular pieces displayed at ASUR are smaller versions of *aksus (or ajsus),* decorative overskirt panels; a fine aksu is a source of pride and prestige (see page 124). Women of the Jalq'a communities weave and wear wildly patterned aksus that I am enchanted with. Crammed with complex, interlocking, multidirectional red and black (or dark brown) creatures, these pieces are said to be inspired by the weavers' dreams and fantasies. Smiling bats and felines with six legs vie for space between long-legged birds and imaginary toothy beasts with snakes in their bellies.

Conversely, weavings from Tarabuco display images of daily activities in real life. For aksus, coca bags (chuspas), and tourist-destined wall hangings, these weavers use very finely spun, dyed sheep's wool weft threads with a strong but fine cotton warp to show crisp details in the intricate scenes. Whereas the Jalq'a aksus have no visible order, examples from the Tarabuco area have a central panel with birds, animals, and people, bordered with fine geometric bands. Tiny figures go about their business making chicha, harvesting corn, marrying, baking bread, and celebrating the Pujllay fiesta. Weavers in the nearby village of Candelaria make similar aksus and small men's shoulder ponchos but with strictly geometric, symmetrical patterning. In both communities, the red, orange, and yellow versions are for daily use, and the purple, blue, and black colorways are for mourning observance, called *luto*.

For the past 20 or so years, talented men from the Tarabuco area have been learning and employing ancient tapestry techniques to create exciting wall hangings, thanks to a textile development project encouraged by ASUR. They use bright, dyed colors of finely spun sheep's wool to weave fanciful scenes of large, multicolored monsters and mythical gods. Their craftsmanship is impressive: the weave is invariably tight and even, forms have perfect, smooth edges, the back looks the same as the front, and there are no loose ends. Sometimes they weave a river with fish running through the scene; each tapestry is completely unique, and the museum has some masterpieces on display.

Situated in a pretty garden, the museum is peaceful and the relaxed ambiance encourages slow and careful appreciation of the exceptional work. There is an admission fee.

The ASUR Museum shop offers a variety of high-quality wall hangings, belts, bags, and other items. Note that a very fine, intricately woven wall hanging (for example, 14 by 22 inches) can cost hundreds of dollars, assuring that the weavers get fair prices for their backbreaking work. Sales at ASUR directly

A Tarabuco weaver demonstrates at the ASUR Museum shop.

benefit the artisans who live in impoverished agricultural areas of Potosí and Chuquisaca departments, considered the poorest part of Bolivia but a region where its cultures are best preserved.

ADDRESS: Downhill to the right from the Mirador de la Recoleta at Pasaje Iturricha 314, Sucre
www.asur.org.bo
museo@asur.org.bo
TEL: +591 4 6456651 or +591 4 6462194
HOURS: Monday–Saturday, 9 a.m.–12:30 p.m. and 2:30 p.m.–6 p.m.

INCA PALLAY STORE

A very complete selection of fine textiles is also available at the Inca Pallay store in downtown Sucre, at fair-trade prices. Inca Pallay Association is composed of over four hundred weavers in fifteen communities in the Jalq'a and Yampara areas. The group helps the women market their creations and has been instrumental in improving lifestyle conditions in rural hamlets. Look at both the ASUR Museum shop and here at Inca Pallay for your special piece before heading to the Tarabuco Sunday market; compare prices and quality. The hard-to-read Inca Pallay website has lots of good information about the weavings and the people.

ADDRESS: Calle Audiencia 97, Sucre
www.incapallay.org
info@incapallay.org
incapallay@entelnet.bo
TEL: +591 4 6461936

Favorite Hotel in Sucre

Hotel de Su Merced, located within easy walking distance of the main plaza gets my vote for the charming, unique rooms, flower-filled patios, homemade breakfast buffet, and warm, friendly staff. The white, tile-roofed building is a restored family mansion of three stories with twenty-three rooms and superb views over the white city from the highest rooftop terrace.

Several languages are spoken: English, French, and Italian.

> **ADDRESS:** Azurduy Street #16 (between Bolívar and Nicolás Ortiz Streets), Sucre
> www.desumerced.com
> hotel@desumerced.com
> reservas@desumerced.com
> **TEL:** +591 46451355 or +591 46445150

Favorite Restaurants in Sucre

La Taverne has a great chef and his international cuisine tops the list in Sucre for unpretentious dishes, beautifully presented. Succulent steaks with a variety of sauces are a specialty.

> **ADDRESS:** Calle Aniceto Arce 35, Sucre
> www.lataverne.com.bo/
> info@lataverne.com.bo
> **TEL:** +591 46455719
> **HOURS:** Monday–Saturday, 8:30 a.m.–11 p.m.; Sunday, 7 p.m.–10 p.m.

Papavero specializes in Italian cuisine—and super pizzas—but there's a selection of Bolivian dishes too. The set lunch for about $5 is a great deal. They do amazing pasta dishes, too. Enter the building and go up the stairs to the right to dine in an elegant setting with casual, friendly ambiance. It gets rave reviews.

> **ADDRESS:** Calle Estudiantes 1, corner with Plaza 25 de Mayo, Sucre
> **TEL:** +591 72046380
> Facebook: Papavero Ristorante e Pizzeria
> **HOURS:** Daily, 12:30 p.m.–10 p.m.

Woman in typical Tarabuco hat and awayo.

Visiting Sucre and Environs

Candelaria Tours is the oldest travel company in Sucre, in business since 1975; it is reputable, with great guides. The kind owner and her family are from Candelaria so they know Sucre and the Tarabuco area intimately. They arrange longer tours to Potosí, Uyuni salt flats, and other destinations.

They also have basic rooms for overnight stays at their Hacienda Candelaria if you need a place to stay during Pujllay, or if you want to commune with weavers or chill in the peaceful countryside; call or email for reservations. They speak English.

> **ADDRESS:** J.J. Perez #301 Plazuela, Cochabamba
> www.candelariatours.com
> liz@candelariatours.com or karina@candelariatours.com
> info@candelariatours.com (also message Liz from the Facebook page)
> **TEL:** +591 4 6440340 or +591 4 6461661

Best Festival near Sucre, at Tarabuco

Tarabuco is a small town at 10,740 feet (3,273 m) in the Andes of central Bolivia, about 40 miles (64 km) southeast of Sucre; it's renowned for the Sunday market and the March festival called Pujllay. Inhabitants are called *Tarabuqueños* but the term refers also to the populations of surrounding villages.

Even though the joyous participatory affair called Pujllay has grown to include national spectators and international tourists, this important festival remains a fascinating celebration to experience—and a great place to see typical textiles in action. On the third Sunday of March, the usually quiet town of Tarabuco fills with villagers, tourists in the know, and urban-dwelling spectators from other towns, all ready to celebrate the 2-day event. The Quechua name means "play" or "celebrate."

Festival beliefs blend mysticism and pagan rituals with observations to honor the ancestors and memorialize a historical event—their hard-won independence over Spanish forces in 1816. People from nearly sixty indigenous Quechua-speaking communities converge from the surrounding countryside to dance and play music in a procession. They give thanks to Pachamama for the fertility of potato crops and for the rain that waters their lands. The most distinctive characteristic of Pujllay is the *pukara*, an enormous ladder-like structure

about 15 feet tall, decoratively and symbolically festooned with foodstuffs such as bread wreaths, net bags of grapes and potatoes, ears of corn, cans of beer, and baggies of coca leaves, all offerings to Pachamama to convince her to send a good harvest. The revelers dance around the pukara and play monotonous flute and drum music for many hours until finally the goodies are doled out to the crowd.

A man from Tarabuco in traditional Pujllay celebration clothing, complete with knitted leggings, tire sandals, and hot pink cape.

Tarabuqueños dress in their most elegant traditional clothing. Men start out with long, loose black *bayeta* woolen tunics, with wide, mid-calf-length white cotton pants underneath. Then they don either of two types of accessories. Some groups of men wear a handwoven burgundy poncho with yellow, red, and green horizonal stripes, tire sandals, and a hard leather *montera* or helmet. Other dancers hang two cotton back panels embroidered with sequins from their shoulders and one or more small square, shoulder ponchos called *kunka unkus* whose quality of intricate woven motifs grant importance and prestige to the wearer. It's interesting to note that woven pieces have warp-faced patterning and four selvedges, that is, they are rarely cut but are woven to size with a circular warp (two identical pieces make a poncho or lliqlla). On top of the small ponchos, these dancers pin incongruous capes of hot pink satin fabric. They decorate their rigid leather monteras with three gathered pieces of tissue paper or cloth, filled with Brillo pad cleaning puffs. They hang several chuspas over their shoulders, and on their feet, they wear the wooden platform sole sandals with oversized metal spurs that will give their feet serious blisters halfway into the festivities. The spurs and the helmet-like monteras, are intended to resemble Spanish conquistador clothing

For festivals, Tarabuqueñas (women) wear a more complex version of everyday dress. An especially fine vertically pleated aksu (or ajsu) is attached with a wide belt over one hip, over a simple black woolen dress called an *almilla*.

Stacks of crocheted and embellished hats traditionally worn by young women in Tarabuco.

Over her shoulders and over the aksu, she drapes a spectacular shawl (manta) or carrying cloth (awayo) and pins it with a *tupu* (shawl pin) or a big safety pin. Women sometimes appropriate the men's black montera or wear a more feminine red wool boat-shaped hat called a *killa*. Pujllay's spectacular rituals, music, and dance performances earned the UNESCO "Intangible Cultural Heritage of Humanity" designation in 2014. The town market is much larger during the festival, and there may be more textiles than usual, so check it out if you are there at this time of year.

Left: An aksu, the anchor of women's traditional dress in the Tarabuco region.

TARABUCO MARKET

For a few dollars each, you can take a shared taxi the 40 miles southeast to Tarabuco, or use Candelaria Tours. Ask at your hotel in Sucre where to find a Tarabuco taxi. Make arrangements the day before because the market starts early.

Once the place to see Tarabuqueños in typical dress at their weekly household market, this event has changed over the years into a tourist textile market. It still has charm, but the locals have mostly decided they are tired of the intrusion. The elders turn their faces from the camera and are not fooled anymore by sneaky long zoom lenses.

But around the main plaza, several dozen textile and craft vendors set up their displays on Sunday mornings, and sometimes they have some excellent new and older woven pieces, both from the immediate area and from other parts of Bolivia. Additionally, all around the plaza permanent shops sell good-quality textiles such as the local men's intricate wool tapestries and the typical Potolo and Ravelo black and red pieces. Some vendors also offer the finely woven red and orange Candelaria and Tarabuco men's ponchos, wall hangings, and small coca bags called chuspas. Even though many of these items such as the wall hangings are made for tourists, you can find superb pieces, finely and carefully woven with traditional motifs. Last time I was there, several vendors had knitted chullos from towns in Potosí Department. (See the explanation of these textiles with the ASUR Museum information, pages 120–121.)

Most of the vendors at the Sunday market are middlemen, so if you have a chance to visit one of the weaving communities, you might be able to buy directly from the weaver, in which case, you will probably be able to photograph her and the family because you have made a friendly connection.

Above: Imaginative depictions of animals and figures from the weaver's dreams are woven into colorful wool Tarabuco tapestries.
Below: Two women draped in handwoven awayos and traditional hats shop for weaving yarn at the Sunday market in Tarabuco.

POTOSÍ

The city of Potosí sits at 13,343 feet (4,067 m), but by the time you get there, you'll probably be well acclimated. It's about one hundred miles (160 km) southwest of Sucre in the central part of Bolivia. Spanish explorers founded Potosí in 1546 next to *Cerro Rico* (Rich Hill) to exploit what they presumed were inexhaustible silver veins. Inca miners had been extracting silver for a century before Spaniards conquered the area, then forced indigenous people to toil underground to dig out the silver. Eventually millions of indigenous and African slaves perished due to the cruel and brutal working conditions of the mines during the three centuries of colonial rule.

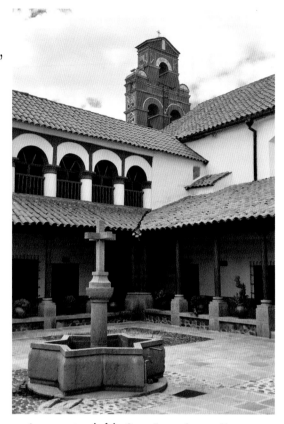

Inner courtyard of the Santa Teresa Convent Museum in Potosí.

The mines of Cerro Rico became the most productive silver mines in the world. Muleteers and their poor beasts hauled thousands of tons of silver ingots over the Andes to the coast and sent it on to Spain. The Spaniards depleted the silver by the end of the seventeenth century. At the same time, with all the available wealth, they built Potosí into a large and important trading city with beautiful colonial churches and imposing mansions—spectacular enough that UNESCO declared it a World Heritage Site.

Potosí has enough redeeming features to justify a visit even if there is not a festival, but the *Ch'utillos* event is great, especially if you miss the Anata Andina and Carnival in Oruro. A visit

to a mine in Cerro Rico is almost mandatory to learn about how the miners still work today; see the ex-miner who does tours, page 129. You'll be outfitted with a slicker, hard helmet with a light, and tall rubber boots because it can be muddy inside. The most interesting feature of mines is the *Tio* or underground deity of the miners; you'll learn about what the miners offer him and why. And be prepared for a potentially gut-wrenching experience as you learn about the history of these mines.

You can see the usual main city sights in a day, but if you are adventurous and want to take a local bus out of Potosí to villages such as Macha (3 hours north) for a market or patron saint's day, you'll find people making merry in traditional textiles and clothing. The village *comparsas* (dancer/musician groups) who gather for local festivities often wear striking regional versions of typical dress.

Getting to Potosí

The easiest way to get to Potosí is to fly into Sucre from La Paz. The airline **Boliviana De Avicion** has a nonstop daily flight and many other flights with stops. Then you can get a bus or shared taxi to Potosí. The almost 100-mile (160 km) ride takes at least 4 hours over paved roads. From any destination, it's best to travel to Potosí in the daylight. The landscape over the winding roads into the city will surprise you with its stark beauty. The route twists and turns through hill and valley, so if you have a tendency to motion sickness, take precautions. Potosí has a new bus station where you will probably end up, inconveniently over a mile (2 km) outside of town, but shared taxis (60 to 75 cents) ply the route back and forth into town. Overnight buses from La Paz to Potosí and back are available several times a day, especially in the evening; the advantage is that you don't pay for a hotel and the obvious drawback is no amazing scenery.

Best Festival in Potosí

The biggest festival in Potosí is called Ch'utillos, or the Festival of San Bartolomé, and it's a great textile event. Ch'utillos takes place on August 24, 25, and 26. It has roots in the indigenous community as well as the Catholic celebrations

Stark and rugged landscape on the road to Potosí.

of Saint Bartholomew's Day. This is a good place to see local festival costume; normally, you'll see the most textiles on the first day, but they could change the program and order of dancing. Some groups that perform wear glitzy satin costumes similar to those in Oruro, but in Potosí, many indigenous groups of villagers also come into town to dance at the main event. Men from a nearby area, who are either dancing, playing in the bands, or hanging around watching, wear the typical fine-gauge black chullos with rows of white stylized "coca flowers." They also wear handknitted leggings with diamond patterns, knit in either brown and ecru wool or brilliant acrylic yarns. You'll surely see women with handwoven carrying cloths or awayos distinctive to each region and others wearing long-sleeved (usually black) dresses called almillas with intricate white machine stitching on the cuffs and hem from Calcha, or others with square blue velvet hats with

Detail of a superfine handknitted chullo from Potosí.

little metal shapes, from a town called Jura. The town fills up for Ch'utillos, so be sure to reserve a hotel well in advance.

Shopping

An artisans' market and a couple of other places in Potosí have interesting textiles from the surrounding towns and communities. Some artisan vendors sell at the Mercado Artesanal on Omiste and Sucre Streets. A few shops along Calle Sucre sell textiles and handicrafts.

Arte Nativo is a project that involves about six hundred rural women from high-altitude hamlets in twenty-four workshops with the goal of improving living conditions for their families. Valuing their own cultural heritage and learning self-esteem sometimes becomes almost as important as making money for food and clothing. They knit and weave items to sell with the fibers from their own sheep, llamas, and alpacas. They could use a volunteer to help design a good website and consistently update it with available products.

ADDRESS: Calle Sucre 30-32
www.artenativobolivia.com
arnativo@cotapnet.com.bo
+591 26223544

Artesanias Palomita's on Avenida Serrudo is full of costumes and textiles, some for sale and others part of a private collection, all interesting.

HOURS: Monday–Saturday, 9 a.m.– noon and 2:30 p.m.–6 p.m.

Vivid colors in this handwoven belt from Potosí show traditional motifs as well as current events: note the tank with the soldier and his machine gun.

Favorite Hotel

Hacienda Cayara is a lovely hotel in a beautiful green valley about 35 minutes from Potosí. In 1557, Hacienda Cayara was the first country estate to be established in "New Toledo," now Bolivia; it still includes a working dairy. The wonderful homey ambiance of the hacienda, with its roaring fireplace, original paintings, and antique furniture invites the visitor to relax and stay a while. A new section of comfortable rooms with private bathrooms has been built for travelers. The manager, David, speaks English and is very welcoming. Breakfast is included and basic country fare for lunch and dinner is available if ordered in advance. You will need a taxi or private transport to get out to Cayara; ask David for help with transportation.

TEL: +591 71497316 (English-speaking)
cayara.reservations@gmail.com for reservations
www.hotelmuseocayara.com/en/home/

Favorite Restaurants in Potosí

Cafe Potocchi is the most popular place in Potosí, serving pasta, llama and other meats, soups, and more, with some vegetarian and vegan options. The owner is friendly; it's a small place so it's good to have reservations or come earlier than most Bolivians eat dinner—before 7:30 to 8 p.m.

ADDRESS: Millares 13, Potosí
TEL: +591 63752789

4060 Restaurant is spacious and casual with very good food, including burgers, pasta, soups, and pizza as well as some Bolivian and vegetarian specialties. (4,060 is how many meters above sea level you are in Potosí.)

ADDRESS: Hoyos 1, Potosí
TEL: +591 2 6222623

And when in Potosí, try the *salteñas* (like an empanada), said to be the best in Bolivia. I love these hot, juicy baked pastry crescents. The succulent meat variety is stuffed with chopped beef and bits of veggies and hard-boiled egg, an olive, and a few raisins. Salteñas are also made with chicken and are great boxed up for a picnic or just eaten on a park bench. Walking around town, you will surely run into one of the many bakery-type places that make fresh salteñas for about 60 cents each. Or ask a local, "Salteñas?" and someone will point you in the right direction.

Visit a Mine

Ex-miner Antonio of **Potochij Tours**, is highly recommended for a visit to the mines.

ADDRESS: Calle Lanza 36, Potosí
@potochjitoursbolivia
Facebook: Potochji Tours
potochijtoursbolivia.wordpress.com
TEL: +591 2 6230625

Above: Typical red and black weaving from the Potolo area near Potosí.
Below: Displays of wall hangings for sale in the Tarabuco market.

FESTIVALS and CELEBRATIONS

In addition to Carnival, Anata Andina, and Ch'utillos, there are numerous celebrations in Bolivia where you are most likely to see an array of textiles, costumes, and processions.

January 6
Dia de los Reyes/Three Kings' Day

The town of Achocalla, 45 to 55 minutes from La Paz, sits in a sweeping green agricultural valley with snow-capped mountain vistas. It holds a big celebration for Dia de los Reyes or Three Kings' Day (Epiphany), which relates to the visit of the three wise men. Chutas dancers twirl with their partner cholitas who are wearing their best macramé shawls and layers of full skirts. The men wear matching fancy pants and jackets decorated with sequins and embroidery; they also wear a screen mask with a knitted chullo, and a big sombrero. In Achocalla, they dance, whirl, and drink on a big flat field and eat traditional foods. Other bigger Reyes festivals with more dance groups are in villages around Oruro, Cochabamba, Sucre, and Tarija.

February 2
Virgen de la Candelaria/Virgin of Candelmas

This day is celebrated throughout Bolivia but especially in Copacabana near Lake Titicaca as well as in Aiquile (Cochabamba), Angostura (Tarija), Challapampa (Oruro).

The Virgen de Copacabana (also called Virgen de la Candelaria, Our Lady of Copacabana) is the patron saint of Bolivia and she is honored in a huge festival in the town plaza. Early in the morning on February 2nd, believers take flower offerings to the lake to ensure good harvests. Later that day, a huge festival takes place in the plaza in front of Copacabana's Moorish-style cathedral. On August 5, the celebration happens all over again, so you might hit on either event in your

Cholitas dance in the Three Kings' Day celebration.

A festival celebrant in Oruro wears the traditional knitted leggings with tire sandals and spurs. The spurs are intended to resemble the dress of Spanish conquistadors.

travels. Our Lady of Copacabana, also known as the Virgin of the Lake, is revered for a series of miracles she is believed to have performed, such as saving fishermen from drowning. A replica statue of the original is brought out in a procession with a lot of cholitas and other dancers. I love watching the priest who comes out of the cathedral to bless the new and newly purchased cars and trucks lined up out front; he spends a bit of time with each car as it pulls forward in line. The owners stand by to open the hood, then the priest dips a carnation into a can of holy water and shakes it three times over the engine as he says a few words to ward off blown gaskets, radiator leaks, and so forth.

Men carry the body of Christ in a glass coffin through the streets of La Paz on Holy Thursday.

You can see the Virgin's statue in the cathedral; also check out the immense hand-carved wooden doors at the entrance that depict local legends. All around the plaza vendors sell red, yellow, and green plastic decorations for cars and homes. Be careful of pickpockets in crowds at this particular event; it has a reputation. Bolivians blame the Peruvians who come over the border, moaning, "Oh, those wily Peruvians!" and vice versa at the Puno event. It's an interesting and casual festival; just don't bring anything that can be stealthily removed from your person— think cross-body purses and hidden waist pouches.

February or March, varies by year
Carnaval/Carnival

In the tropical city of Santa Cruz de la Sierra, there is a different sort of Carnaval, more like the Brazilian affair in Rio. Dancers wear fancy, glittery and often scanty costumes with lots of feathers. Many of the elaborate costumes have large extensions or wings and the dancers ride on floats. Exciting and pretty, but there is no indigenous aspect.

March or April, varies by year
Semana Santa/Holy Week or Easter Week

Semana Santa, or Holy Week, is the week leading up to, but not including, Easter Sunday. You may be able to see some textiles or traditional dress during this event in small villages but city people dress in street clothes. The week is interesting as a cultural event, and most towns hold some form of religious observances during these days. In general the observances seem far more serious than in Peru. In Sucre, all the beautiful churches are open on Thursday and the priests use the occasion to renew their vows. In many places, twelve special traditional dishes are eaten, including *papas rellenas* (mashed potato stuffed with chopped meat and vegetables) and *arroz con leche* (a rice and milk drink). On Holy Thursday in La Paz, men with alarming pointed cloth hoods and long purple robes carry the crucified body of Christ in a glass coffin along the streets. Pilgrims walk 150 km from La Paz to Copacabana to climb the hill called *Cerro Calvario* and repent on Good Friday at the twelve Stations of the Cross that overlook the town.

May 3
Fiesta de la Cruz/
Festival of the Cross

Celebrated on the Island of Suriqui (Lake Titicaca), Tarija, Copacabana, Achacachi, Tarabuco, Macha, and Cochabamba, this festival celebrates the cross on which Christ was crucified, but significance of the sacrifice is more to the point. All the towns listed have celebrations with dancing and music. In Macha (Potosí Department), this is a major festival with pre-Christian significance and almost no Christian impact today. (The Spaniards cleverly integrated Catholic holidays with ancient rituals to marginally convert rural people.) On the main day, a mass is read in Aymara and food and drink are shared. After dancing for some hours, the *Tinku* or ritual hand-to-hand fighting begins, with a violence intended to release anger and solve communal conflicts. In the past, the communities fought until someone died and their blood was offered to Pachamama to ensure a

fruitful harvest. And although the government attempts to prohibit Tinku, gravely injured or dead combatants still result from the ritual, especially because drinking alcohol is also part of the tradition. Macha itself is a better place to see a Tinku than a little village because it is a fairly large town where tourists are not rare. But if you are a female traveling alone, it might be better to visit Macha and other towns in the area when it's market day, not during a festival. Market day in Macha is Sunday. The women of the Macha area are superb weavers and the men make fine chullos. In this area, men also make machine-embroidered jackets and checked woven scarves that are part of their outfits.

In Tarabuco for the Festival of the Cross, the people carry three crosses in procession. The first and largest one is covered in beautiful fabrics, the second, medium-sized cross is covered in handwoven awayos, and the third is a little stone cross decorated with an image of Christ. Each one is blessed by the local priest at each corner of the plaza. Like the Tarabuco festival of Pujllay, the Festival of the Cross traditions require that participants wear their richly colored and handmade clothing.

Young men carry the cross adorned in handwoven cloth through the streets of Macha during the Festival of the Cross. Above: A man in traditional dress during the Festival of the Cross in Macha.

Late May to early June
La procesión del Gran Poder/ The Procession of the Great Power of Jesus

This huge festival in La Paz city commemorates Christ the All Powerful and a miraculous painting of the Holy Trinity. Initiated in the 1930s with a simple candlelight procession, Gran Poder has evolved into an enormous street festival with 30,000 dancers and musicians, and far more spectators. Roads along the parade route are blocked off and bleachers set up so everyone can see. Celebrants solemnly carry the painting through town, followed by a procession of 65 or more dance groups in elaborate matching costumes accompanied by loud brass marching bands. Popular with both La Paz's non-indigenous population and with the Aymara people, Gran Poder

Pepinos cavort with Chutas dancers during the Procession of the Great Power.

crowds get bigger every year. Costumes and music are similar to Carnival in Oruro with groups such as the Morenada and *Kullaguadas*, but there are roles and groups that don't perform in Oruro such as the *Doctorcitos* and the *Pepinos* or clowns. The juxtaposition of tipsy adult clowns cavorting in a supposedly religious procession may surprise you, but Bolivians seamlessly mix merry-making with Aymara folklore and Catholic observances. (Note that this is not a good day to arrive in or leave La Paz because roads are blocked or congested in the central part of town.)

August 14
*Virgen de Urkupiña/*Virgin of Urkupiña

The festival of the Virgin of Urkupiña in Quillacollo (Cochabamba) commemorates the legend about the Virgin turning rocks into pure silver for a poor little girl. Today, the celebration attracts nearly half a million people each year who come to ask favors of the Virgin. The festival begins with a parade with the saint paraded in front of over 10,000 dancers and musicians. Many groups dance here, such as the Diablada, the Morenada, and others unique to this festival. Following the immense parade, a mass takes place, which is a solemn event that ends with a march of the image of the Virgin of Urkupiña through the Quillacollo streets. The festival ends with a procession up the hillside where traditions says that the Virgin appeared. Food and miniatures are sold, and dancing and music go on all night.

August 15
*Virgen de la Asunción/*Virgin of the Assumption

Known more for its mines than its festivals, Llallagua (Oruro) really knows how to celebrate, perhaps because life here is monotonous and monochromatic most of the year. The people here observe the Assumption with Catholic mass, processions, and fireworks in addition to dancing to music played on wooden instruments. And for fiestas the revelers wear colorful handmade clothing. Both men and women in this dusty mining town weave and knit brilliant belts and chullos. Both types of textiles are made with the finest acrylic (probably overspun), with complex patterns of birds, and in nearby Lagunillas with geometric patterning.

August 16
Fiesta de San Roque/Festival of San Roque

The feast day of San Roque, the patron saint of dogs (and originally, of plague victims), is officially on the 16th of August, but in the town of Tarija a week-long San Roque celebration begins on the first Sunday in August. Sculpted figures of the saint always show him with a dog at his right side. In some towns, San Roque protects dogs and unmarried people.

In Tarija, the saint is better known for protecting not only dogs but also the poor and the ill. He is said to have cured plague victims and believers still pray to him for cures. The saint's figure is taken out of the church in procession with thousands of dancers dressed as the native Chapacos of Tarija—mestizos of Spanish and Tomata Indian descent—wearing floppy capes, long skirts, shapeless soft cloth masks, and a thick circle of feathers around a wide headband. The Chapacos parade through the streets to the music of drums, flutes, and very long horns. After visiting hospitals along the route, San Roque is returned to the church. In many towns, the celebration in San Roque's honor involves decorating dogs with ribbons on all four paws. Modern animal lovers use the occasion to make the townspeople aware of abandoned and mistreated dogs. This fiesta is also celebrated in La Paz and Cochabamba.

Late August to early September
Virgen de Santa Rosa/Virgin of Santa Rosa

Yotala, a small town near Sucre, celebrates its patron saint, Santa Rosa, all week before the final folkloric dancing and processions on September 2nd. The festival ends on September 4th with a final bullfight in a small arena.

September 8 (or the weekend closest to this date)
Virgen de Guadalupe or *Mamita de Guadalupe*/Virgin of Guadalupe

The Virgin of Guadalupe is the patron saint of many towns such as Sucre and Viacha (La Paz). Sucre goes all out to venerate the Virgin, with a festival that includes a two-day parade with Morenadas, Diabladas, Llameros, Caporales, Tobas, Tinkus and Tarabuqueño dancers (many of the same groups as at Oruro Carnival). Add to that one brass band for each bloque or sub-group, and lots of loud fireworks; your ears will be ringing for hours. The painting of the Virgin is taken around town in procession and returned to her chapel, near Sucre's Metropolitan Cathedral. Pilgrims from all over Bolivia and the world visit her shrine. In an interesting twist on the cargamentos of Oruro, Sucre's Central Market vendors decorate cars with fruits and vegetables and stuffed animals and dolls. They snake through town and back to the market, creating traffic jams in their wake. As with most festivals, there are many pop-up kitchens along the street with fried chicken and French fries and snacks. If you didn't make it to Oruro's Carnival, the Guadalupe celebration has many of the same elements, at a lower, warmer altitude. The Tinkus and the Tarabuco dancers wear typical textiles as part of their costumes.

Appendix

TRANSPORTATION ADVICE FOR PERU AND BOLIVIA

Thieves love to hang out at bus and train stations in Peru and Bolivia. They will distract you for a second by dropping a bunch of coins on the ground, for instance, while someone else grabs your bag and is out the door and gone before you have time to react. They are good (or bad) at what they do, and they do it very quickly. Keep your luggage between your feet with a foot through the strap or your hand on the handle at all times.

For safety reasons, I recommend flying anywhere you can, if you can afford it; flights are reasonably priced and save a lot of time. If you don't want to fly, then I recommend Peru Hop and Bolivia Hop buses.

Read the information on the websites before you book any bus trips. I don't want to scare you, but I want you to have all the facts. There have been a few bus hijackings over the Andes in recent years, statistically very few compared to all the trips driven, but nevertheless worth knowing about so you are prepared. The robbers block the road with rocks and stop the bus. They board and take everything; they know all about our clever neck or waist passport holders and so will demand those, too. But they don't go into the mounds of luggage stored below the bus because there isn't time and they have already gotten loads of wonderful things just from the tourists' carry-on bags. Travel by train is safer than a bus trip.

www.peruhop.com/traveling-by-bus-in-peru/
www.peruhop.com/peru-hop-vs-public-buses-in-peru/

At bus and train stations, you might encounter anything from a clean modern café to an older

woman with a bucket of chicha and some dirty, used glasses. Use common sense. When the bus or train stops at a station, vendors usually come on board to sell inexpensive homemade foods like papas rellenas, those balls of mashed potato stuffed with chopped meat and vegetables and then fried. They are delicious, but it's better not to add the extra (uncooked) sauce you may be offered. The food vendors usually have their offerings in baskets with a clean cloth over the top and they hand you the food with a clean piece of paper. Whip out some Kleenex or toilet paper for napkins. Sometimes they sell food, drinks, and crafts through the open bus or train windows, a good reason to always have a pocket of small change handy.

Watch your belongings in the confusion of vendors boarding and exiting buses or trains. Naturally, you need to keep your possessions in view while people roam back and forth in the aisle; don't put your expensive camera under your seat or above your head where you can't see it. Most trains and buses for tourists are very safe, but in local transport, you might be traveling with tempting items that are worth more than the average occupant earns in a month or a year. If you go to sleep on a bus, be sure your valuables can't be taken without you waking up; wrap your arm through a strap or whatever. I don't want to be an alarmist; I just want you to be careful. I have had something stolen only twice in over forty visits to the Andean countries, while the times that strangers in chullos or bowler hats have helped me or shared their food are innumerable.

Peru

For the past two decades, I have traveled around Peru and Bolivia either in a private van or on domestic flights with my group tours. But this winter, I took a Cruz del Sur bus to Huancayo, Peru (no airport there), and was very happy with the efficient ticket sales, clean bus stations, and comfortable travel experience. These large buses have only three seats across in each row, two together on the left side of the aisle, and one on the right. I had a single reclining seat by the window, and I read a book, looked at the scenery, and slept with the included blanket and pillow. Long-distance buses such as Cruz del Sur usually offer a little airplane-style meal and cookies on the nonstop routes, or you can bring some favorite snacks.

The particular route I took has not had hijackings, but they do happen on the Lima to Cusco route that goes over the Andes. If you want to take a bus to Cusco from Lima, make sure it goes the southern safer (and longer) route to Arequipa and Puno and then north to Cusco. Daytime buses are safer than night buses. There is good advice about buses on the Peru Hop website to encourage you to go with them, of course, but they really are safer.

I recommend the following bus companies as long as you buy tickets for the southern route; check

The road from Cusco to Puno travels over La Raya Pass at heights of more than 14,000 feet.

the map. There are also local bus companies that are less expensive, less comfortable, and less safe than the four listed below.

Best Peruvian Bus Companies (for long-distance travel)
CRUZ DEL SUR

VIP or regular double-deck buses are clean and modern, with heat and air-conditioning, bathroom, seat belts, movies on personal video screens, snacks, and an onboard assistant. The single or double reclining seats are huge, very comfortable, and come with a blanket and pillow. Theoretically, you can buy tickets and choose your seat online, but the website doesn't always work. To solve the problem, the company has several sales points around Lima where you can purchase your tickets, and they accept credit cards; see the website for locations. If traveling alone and you want peace and quiet, choose from the row of single window seats on the right side of the bus. Cruz del Sur goes everywhere in Peru and even to Argentina, Chile, and other South American cities. See the website (in English) for current routing and departure times.

ADDRESS: Avenida Javier Prado 1109, La Victoria, Lima
www.cruzdelsur.com.pe
TEL: +51 1 3115050

PERU HOP BUS
Peru Hop buses come highly recommended; I have no personal experience with the company, started by two young Irish guys, but the concept is great. They pick you up at your hotel (or a nearby meeting point if you are outside the city)

and drop you at the next one, so you avoid the bus stations entirely. They offer relatively inexpensive bus passes that include scheduled, guided stops at interesting sights along the way. And you can get off, stay a while, and board the next bus a week or a month later. It is a great idea that I wish someone had thought of 30 years ago! The company website says, "We pride ourselves on having passengers from every corner of the world. No matter your nationality or age, if you're solo or with a group, family or couple, all are welcome. Our bilingual guides also make the journey more fun." Check out their information before making any bus plans.

www.peruhop.com
TEL: +51 1 2422140

EXPRESO MOLINA

Expreso Molina Bus Company has four classes of modern, double-deck buses with heat and air-conditioning, reclining seats, bathroom, video monitors, onboard assistant, snacks on long routes, blankets, and pillows. Molina has some different routes and departures and all the itineraries are nonstop.

ADDRESS: Nicolás Ayllón 1352, San Luis, Lima (Yerbateros)
www.molinaunion.pe
reserva@molinaunion.pe
TEL: +51 1 7190274

MIRABUS IN LIMA

In addition to tours down the coast to Pachacamac, the good Mirabus company also offers tours that include the district of Miraflores,

Young girl from Accha Alta, Peru, plies yarn she has just spun.

classic Lima city tours by day and night, a tour to the Larco Museum, as well as a Peruvian dinner and show tour.

The ticket booth and departure point are at Parque Kennedy, Miraflores.

www.mirabusperu.com/
reservas@mirabusperu.com
TEL: +51 1 2426699

Bolivia

Taxi

Taxis are inexpensive in La Paz and around Bolivia. I don't roam around alone at night, but I have never had a problem with a taxi driver in Peru or Bolivia. However, most don't have or use meters so agree on the price with the driver before you get in. Radio taxis (vehicles clearly labeled, with radio communication) are the safest; they can also call in to headquarters to get directions if not sure of an address.

Reputable hotels like the Rosario in La Paz have a guardian/doorman who will hail a taxi and write down the taxi vehicle number as you leave. If your hotel doesn't have someone visible to help, ask someone at the hotel reception desk to find a taxi for you and to write down the number. Hotels all know the drill and naturally want to protect tourists. When finding a taxi elsewhere than in front of your hotel, opt for the radio taxis. A restaurant or even a store will be happy to call a radio taxi for you or put you in a safe taxi with a known driver.

Some taxis charge per person so be sure to ask the total price. Taxis are usually more expensive (also in Peru) at night or the wee hours of the morning. If something makes you uneasy at first glance, don't get in. If you are already in, take out your cell phone and have an imaginary conversation in English so the person knows you have communication (this ploy works all over the world). Most taxi drivers are very helpful and eager to be appreciated. If you speak a bit of Spanish, you can practice some questions and have a good conversation with a bored driver.

Long routes from city to city, such as Sucre to Potosí, for example, can be done by private taxi more conveniently, for around US$7 to $10 per person, with a few requested stops for photos and bathroom breaks (in the bush, most likely). If two to four people get together and hire a vehicle and driver (taxis only hold four), you will be comfortable and they are quite affordable. Ask your hotel for a recommendation. Collective taxis called *trufis* leave from most bus stations and are cheap and good for short routes, but you might be crammed between strangers in the middle of the back seat for interminable hours; it depends on the circumstances. For a long trip through remote areas, I wouldn't go with a completely unknown driver so ask at your hotel or a local travel agency for a recommended person. Once recently, when roads were blocked by a strike, I took an 11-hour taxi ride over the alternative route through absolute wilderness with a pleasant young driver, but I had found him through a local travel agency, so I felt comfortable.

Bus

Flota is the generic name for buses, sometimes incorporated into the company name. Try to take daytime buses because the scenery is incredible on all the routes and it is much safer. All routes except La Paz to Oruro are very sinuous; take Dramamine or other motion sickness prevention

meds. If you are doing a long route such as La Paz to Sucre or Potosí, most lines have *cama* (bed) reclining seats that are very comfortable. Depending on how many hours you will be in the bus, and its quality, of course, take water and snacks/food and a warm jacket, warm shoes and socks, and a wool cap, especially if traversing the Andes or altiplano at night. Some fancy buses give you snacks, a pillow, and blanket, but there could be times when the heat doesn't work or the windows don't open and you will be sweltering. Even an upscale bus could have a rare breakdown and it will be very cold in the Andes. Console yourself that the scenery is like no other.

Bolivia Hop is the same good company that also services Peru (see page 137). It goes from La Paz to Copacabana and/or Puno and Cusco (where it becomes Peru Hop), and back. This service allows you to hop on or off at any of these places, and the bilingual guide on board will assist at the border. Hop arrives in Copacabana from La Paz with the usual hour-long stop to go through Immigration/ Customs, then offers options to visit the Island of the Sun when on the Bolivian side. It's all explained on the website: www.boliviahop.com

DIRECT BUS ROUTES

The good part about buses in Bolivia is that all companies leave from the same bus terminal in any given city, so you can shop around, read the big signs, and see what prices and vehicles look like. There may be hawkers shouting out the destinations to entice you to use that company; ignore them until you find what you want.

For direct routes from one place to another, you can try the bus-finder website **Tickets Bolivia:** www.ticketsbolivia.com, but it doesn't show all the direct routes nor all the good recommended companies. The site seems like such a great idea, but the site consolidates information for only some bus companies. I suspect the omitted companies aren't willing to pay whatever percentage they charge for the booking. For example, there are dozens and dozens of daily direct buses from La Paz to Oruro, but Tickets Bolivia only shows a few direct routes; the rest have crazy schedules, like starting in La Paz, going hours out of your way to Uyuni, then back north to Oruro. Read the site carefully to avoid a long stopover somewhere you didn't plan to visit.

If you find a *direct* route online, see their FAQ section. Book tickets 48 hours in advance, and pay with PayPal or Stripe. Customers have the quite amazing choice of payment in one of twenty-six currencies and the ability to check out in fifteen different languages—presuming all of that works. You'll get an electronic link to your ticket that you can show from your phone or tablet when you board with your passport. It sounds to me like an ambitious, optimistic idea that will work better when the country has better technology. Many places have no Wi-Fi, and if your phone or tablet battery dies, there is no place to charge it to allow you to show your electronic ticket.

The recommended method is to buy tickets for nonstop routes at the bus station on departure day or the day before. Buy your bus tickets a few days in advance during holidays and Carnival; seats do sell out at those times.

POPULAR BUS ROUTES

Note that the one-way bus routes described here are only a guideline, and all buses go back the way they came. I suggest you check at the bus station or a travel agency for accurate, current schedules. (Dramamine or a similar medication is recommended for all Andean bus routes.)

BUS FROM LA PAZ TO ORURO: 144 miles (232 km), 3.5–4 hours

This flat route over the altiplano is paved all the way and is an easy, pleasant ride. A dozen or more companies leave La Paz every 30 minutes for Oruro and more frequently during Carnival to accommodate all the dancers and musicians who come from Santa Cruz, Cochabamba, and elsewhere.

Flota TransCopacabana is excellent and **Andina, Avaroa**, and **Naser** are also recommended.

BUS FROM LA PAZ TO SUCRE: 431 miles (694 km), 12 hours

This is an overnight route with flat reclining seats on Flota TransCopacabana; US$25.

BUS FROM LA PAZ TO TARIJA: 546 miles (878 km), 11 hours

Flota San Lorenzo operates a bus from La Paz to Tarija twice daily. Tickets cost $36 and the journey takes about 11 hours. Three other operators also service this route. Boliviana de Aviación flies from La Paz to Tarija three times daily.

BUS FROM SUCRE TO ORURO: 300 miles (483 km), 7–8+ hours

This is another paved route with many twists and turns through the valleys and over the altiplano; most buses stop in Potosí for a break. US$7 for a regular bus seat; US$15–$25 for reclining seats, which you will probably want because all the buses leave at night.

BUS FROM POTOSÍ TO ORURO: 200 miles (322 km), 6 hours over a winding road

There are two daily direct buses from Potosí to Oruro and back with **Trans-Azul** for less than US$5. If leaving from Potosí, you'll depart from the new terminal (*Nueva Terminal*) which is located 20 minutes from the town center; taxis to the bus terminal are less than US$1.

BUS FROM POTOSÍ TO SUCRE: 96 miles (155 km), 3–4 hours scenic journey over a paved road

There are seven daily direct buses to Sucre and back for US$3. **TransEmperador** or **El Dorado** are recommended.

Check the **Buses Bolivia** website for TransEmperador routes:

www.busesbolivia.wordpress.com/2016/03/03/trans-emperador/

Carnival celebrant in Oruro, Bolivia.

TRAIN
Regular train and Ferrobus services out of Oruro only go south to Uyuni and Tupiza, towns which are not included in this book.

AIRLINES
Boliviana de Aviación and **Amaszonas** both have modern planes and good schedules. Boliviana de Aviación has one nonstop from La Paz to Sucre and seven to eight more flights all day long with a stop in Cochabamba for $200. It's possible to fly into all major cities except Potosí.

GLOSSARY

A glossary of terms used in this book identified by language. A: Aymara; Q: Quechua; S: Spanish.

Aksu (Q.) Handwoven panel or overskirt, usually about 24-30 inches wide, worn on one side over a woman's hip or backside. The aksu is usually worn on top of a long-sleeved dress called an almilla. The Aksu is secured with a belt worn in parts of central Bolivia— Potosí and Chuquisaca Departments.

Almilla (Sp.) Loose, long-sleeved dress usually made of black handwoven cloth; worn by women in northern and central Bolivia. Other clothing is often worn on top, such as an aksu and a belt. In some places almillas are decorated with machine embroidery, for example, almillas from Calcha have intricate white flowery patterns on the sleeves.

Anata Andina (A.) A festival celebrated in the Bolivian highlands, evolved from pre-Hispanic rituals. Linked to the agricultural cycle, it is celebrated every year in the rainy season, during the month of February.

Aniline Dye Dye invented in the mid-1800s by an 18-year-old in England while trying to synthesize quinine to prevent malaria. He synthesized coal-burning residue called coal tar, and the first color was a stunning mauve.

A stack of handwoven awayos in a mix of wool and acrylic.

Awayo (A.) Square carrying cloth made from two handwoven rectangles stitched together down the middle. People fold it in half diagonally, tie the ends in front and use it as a backpack to carry babies, orphaned baby animals, vegetables, and just about any other item.

Bayeta (Sp.) Handwoven cloth, made on treadle looms by men and used for clothing in rural areas. Bayeta is usually made of handspun sheep's wool; black, white, and red are most common colors.

Bloques (Sp.) One part of a larger Carnival dance group or "block.'" For instance a Diablada dance group might have bloques from several different towns or neighborhoods.

Caporales Dancers (Sp.) Carnival dance groups that originally represented mestizo overlords or bosses on the slave plantations. Today the only remnant of these origins is a rawhide latigo that the men carry, but never unroll. The Caporales men and woman wear elaborately embroidered, multicolored, satin and sequin costumes, often with foam-stuffed shoulder extensions. The females' skirts are very short and the choreography involves a lot of twirling in platform high heels. The men's boots have 10-12 tin bells that jingle when they dance and jump in their electric performances. Along with the devil dancers, it is the most popular group at Carnival.

Cargamentos (Sp.) The decorated cars driven in Carnival processions on Saturday, in Oruro. Silver platters, tureens, plates and spoons are attached to brightly colored cloths covering the cars. The silver is said to represent the riches that the Spaniards took from Bolivia, now offered to the Virgin of the Mineshaft.

Cañihua (Sp.) Highly nutritious, teeny brown grain of the quinoa family, *Chenopodium pallidicaule*, also kaniwa. Very resilient, grows at higher altitudes than quinoa.

Cargamentos in Bolivia.

Cherimoya (*Annona cherimola*), also spelled chirimoya. Also called Alligator or Dinosaur Fruit, a prehistoric-looking, green, irregularly oval fruit with sweet white flesh and large black inedible seeds.

Chicha (Q.) Homemade beer in both Peru and Bolivia. Can be made from corn, barley, kiwicha, etc.; sometimes fruit such as strawberries are added.

Chiriuchu (Q.) Spicy guinea pig, chicken, sausage, and corn

Cholitas (Sp.) Young Aymara-speaking indigenous or mestiza women from Bolivia, especially from the La Paz area, who wear typical dress of gathered skirt (pollera), blouse or cardigan, a silky fringed shawl called a manta, and often an apron or delantal. They typically wear several petticoats called enaguas. Discriminated against for decades because they often work for a pittance or for room and board as nannies or maids, cholitas are now standing up for their rights to an education and recognition as valuable citizens.

Chullo or Ch'ullu (Q.) Lluchu (A.) Handknitted cap with pointed or rounded top, of wool, alpaca or acrylic yarns. Most often worn by men and often knitted by men also.

Chumpi (Q.) A wide handwoven belt

Chuspa (Q.) Handwoven coca pouch, usually with a little pocket called a wawa or baby, woven in to hold the lejia, a combination of ash and potato and/or sugar, as a catalyst to activate the alkalis in the leaves.

Chutas dance Typical dance from the La Paz area, performed at Carnival time and for other local festivals. Chutas dance steps involve dizzying twirling. Women wear bowler hats, fancy full skirts and fancy, fringed, velveteen jackets with cardboard-stiffened peplums. Jacket fronts and sleeves are often patterned with beads and complex designs made from soutache braid. Men wear decorated jackets and matching pants, with screen masks. Clowns called Pepinos cavort among the dancers wearing two-color satin costumes and satin masks with curved horns.

Ch'utillos (Sp.) Most important festival in Potosí honoring St. Bartholomew and featuring thousands of dancers, especially the local Tinku groups; August 24–26.

Comparsa (Sp.) Dance group at Carnival

Diablada (Sp.) The dance of the Devils, the first Carnival dance group, initiated in the early 1900s. Devil dancers wear large tin masks, or masks made with a felt base, augmented with cloth and papier-mâché with mirror embellishment and light bulbs for eyes. Women dressed in feminine devil outfits with short skirts perform as Diablesas; all dancers wear elaborately embroidered capes, chest plates and panels over long-sleeved shirts with matching leggings. Special matching boots are made by hand for the devils and also for most of the other dance groups.

Encomienda (Sp.) A Spanish colonial system of control of the indigenous populations, much like feudalism. Spaniards who were supposed to protect and convert the local people instead demanded tribute and forced labor.

Granadilla (Sp.) Oval, egg-shaped orange fruit about the size of a large plum, native to the Andes. Eaten by breaking it in two around the middle and spooning or slurping out the grayish flesh. Very delicious; with small seeds that can be crunched like pomegranate seeds. (I convert a few people to loving granadilla on every trip.)

Jalq'a (Q.) General name for the people and textiles of Potolo and Ravelo areas of Chuquisaca Department, Bolivia

Kiwicha (Q.) High protein, very small grain similar to quinoa, bright cerise in the field; amaranth family. Served often at breakfast, it is puffed, like puffed-rice cereal.

Lancha (Sp.) General term for a small motorboat, on Lake Titicaca for example.

Lliqlla (Q.) Square or rectangular carrying cloth made from two handwoven rectangles stitched together down the middle. Worn over the shoulders and pinned in front. Llacota is another word for this type of textile. Called an awayo in Aymara.

Luto (Sp.) Mourning. Some textiles are made especially for wearing while in mourning, such as the purple, blue, and black chuspas and ponchos of Tarabuco.

Mascareros (Sp.) Mask makers, usually men, who fashion various kinds of festival masks of tin or felt and papier maché. Masks must be of the current style to be worn for Carnival or other celebrations such as Gran Poder in La Paz, thus mascareros create full-time.

Manta (Sp.) Mantle. A large rectangular or square cloth, usually handwoven, with regionally-specific motifs and colors. Used by both men and women tied into a bundle to carry things like onions, babies, or orphaned sheep; to put down under market produce; and to protect the wearer from the cold. Bodies of pre-Hispanic nobility were often buried with sumptuous mantles, wrapped around the mummies as if to protect them. In the La Paz area of Bolivia, manta refers to the brocade shawls with the long macramé fringe.

Maquito (Q.) Handknitted, patterned arm warmers, typically used in the Peruvian highlands, worn over shirt sleeves to protect arms from the cold

Montera (Sp.) Traditional women's wool and/or felt hat, with many varied regional characteristics so it's possible to identify a woman's hometown by her hat style. Some are adorned with wide beaded bands or little woven ties.

Morenada (Sp.) Dance of the Morenos, or dark-skinned people. This festival dance role represents the black slaves brought to work in the Potosí mines—and later in the colonists' sugar cane, grape, and tobacco fields in the lowlands.

History claims that the indigenous people were sympathetic with the overworked slaves and banded together with them in the Morenada dance that mocked the Spaniards; the lugubrious music and repetitive steps further the general ambiance of the performance. Original costumes from the early 1900s show the same rigid, barrel-shaped costume worn today, with heavy cardboard jacket and black mask with the distended tongue of an exhausted worker. Morenada masks are still fabricated with a pipe in the mouth ruefully indicating that only the Spaniards smoked the tobacco that the blacks harvested. Dancers carry a ratchet noisemaker that they twirl at specific times in the dance, said to be reminiscent of the cranking of the grape presses. A female role was added to the Morenada at some point, and these dancers wear outfits with elaborate beaded and sequined blouses, very short skirts, and high boots, similar to the Caporales costume.

Obraje (Sp.) Workshop set up by Spaniards where the Inca people worked for little or no pay. Some obrajes were like sweatshops where weavers were forced to make cloth for the conquerors.

Orureño (-a) (Sp.) Person living in or from Oruro, Bolivia

Paceño (-a) (Sp.) Person living in or from La Paz, Bolivia

Pachamama (Q.) Mother Earth, the most important deity for all (predominately animist, marginally Catholic) Andean people. She is regularly offered beer, alcohol, or chicha; even in a restaurant it's not frowned upon to whisk foam from a beer onto the floor for Pachamama. The Anata Andina celebration in Oruro is the grandest expression of giving thanks to Pachamama, for good harvests and fertility of animals and people—and asking her for more of the same.

Polainas (Sp.) Handknitted, woolen ankle-to-knee leg warmers, used mostly in Potosí Department in Bolivia during ritual fighting called Tinku, during outdoor work in freezing weather, or during festivals as part of the costume. Old versions were made of thick black and natural sheep's wool in zigzag patterns, often in a diagonal sprang-type stitch. Nowadays dancers wear polainas knit with multicolored acrylic yarns in ingenious garter-stitch diamonds. For festivals such as Pujllay, men in the Sucre-Tarabuco area wear a shorter, multicolored, patterned version handknit from wool, with thick-soled sandals and spurs.

Polleras (Sp.) Gathered full skirts worn by women in the Andes

Pujllay (Q.) Important festival in Tarabuco, Bolivia, and environs. Celebrates independence from Spaniards and gives thanks to Pachamama. Word means play or dance in Quechua.

Pukara, pucara (Q.) The tall ladder-like structure set up for Pujllay and covered with vegetables, bread rings, and other foods as offerings to Pachamama to ensure good crops next season. Found in Tarabuco and nearby villages of Bolivia.

Quinoa (Q.) High protein, tiny grain that grows at high altitude on stalks that appear orange to red-pink in the fields; *Chenopodium quinoa*, also amaranth family, like kiwicha. Used in soups.

Salteña (Sp.) Baked meat or chicken filled turnovers eaten as mid-morning snacks. Like empanadas but with a richer dough and a sweeter filling, with a few raisins.

Selvedge, **or Selvage** Edges of cloth or fabric.

Soroche (Sp.) Altitude sickness.

Talleres (Sp.) Artisan's workshops, such as the mask makers' and costume embroiderers' studios in Oruro and La Paz.

Tapestry Weaving technique that is weft-faced usually with discontinuous and/or eccentric weft threads. The warp is typically not visible in a finished tapestry, although of course there are many variations of art tapestry. Men in Pitumarca, Peru, have revived pre-Hispanic tapestry techniques, as has Maximo Laura of Ayacucho, now famous for his tapestry work.

Tarabuqueño (-a) (Sp.) Person from the town of Tarabuco.

Tari (A.) Small, square, handwoven cloth with spiritual significance, for coca leaf rituals. Treasured by their owners, often with tassels on the corners; tied into a bundle when carrying coca leaves. If a tari is on the ground with coca leaves on it, it should not be stepped over but should be gone carefully around.

Tinku (Q.) Ritual fight between communities; now also refers to the popular dance groups that wear cowhide helmets with many colorful striped or plaid scarves and diamond-patterned knitted leg warmers.

Tio (Sp.) Uncle, but also the underground god of the miners; every mine has a tio figure. He is propitiated with offerings of coca leaves, cigarettes, and alcohol and protects the miners from cave-ins. If he is angry he can cause cave-ins and accidents in the mines.

Tucumanis (Sp.) Similar snack to salteñas but deep-fried and often served with peanut sauce. Made by vendors who make them at home and sell them only at mid-morning, around offices or universities especially.

Tumbo (Sp.) Small, smooth, yellow fruit shaped like a small mango, with sweet orange pulp and black seeds. Of the genus *Passiflora* so related to passion fruit but native to Andean valleys; tumbos are eaten fresh or made into a delicious ice cream.

RESOURCES
Travel Agencies in Peru
CUSCO

SAS Travel
www.incatrailperutrek.com
TEL: +51 84 249194

Inkayni Peru Tours
www.inkayniperutours.com
TEL: +51 084 597097

Day Hikes and Self-Guided Tours Peru
www.dayhikesperu.com
www.selfguidedperu.com
TEL: +51 084 241705

HUANCAYO

Pakary Travel Tours
www.tourshuancayo.com
contacto@tourshuancayo.com
TEL: +51 06422 4130

Incas del Peru
www.incasdelperu.org
TEL: +51 64 393298
incasdelperu@gmail.com

LAKE TITICACA

Coyla Adventures
www.uros-titicaca.com/
titicaca_guide@yahoo.es
TEL: +51 998867112

Travel Agencies in Bolivia
LA PAZ

Turisbus
www.turisbus.com
TEL: +591 2 2798786

ORURO

Ludora Travel Club
www.boliviatravelsite.com
reservations@boliviatravelsite.com
TEL: +591 4 4582363

SUCRE
Candelaria Tours
www.candelariatours.com
TEL: +591 4 6440340 or +591 4 6461661

Tours in Peru and Bolivia
BEHIND THE SCENES ADVENTURES TEXTILE AND FESTIVAL TOURS
Annual trips to Peru and Bolivia, with Cynthia LeCount Samaké.

Peru Spring Tour
A textile tour adventure from the superb museums and gourmet restaurants of Lima to Andean highland villages with the jungles of Machu Picchu and the beautiful, colonial Cusco in between. Includes an Andean knitting techniques workshop with Cynthia and a village dye workshop with Nilda Callañaupa.

Bolivia Textiles Tour with Carnival Option
Carnival and textile tour to see the best of Bolivia—the intricate weaving and the amazing knitting, a peaceful rural hacienda, historical places, such as colonial Sucre and the famous silver-mining city of Potosí, and the exciting city of La Paz. Ends with the amazing Carnival celebration, with its elaborate costumes, masks, and music.

www.btsadventures.com
info@btsadventures.com
TEL: 925-957-6690 below email address.

PUCHKA PERU CULTURAL TOURS
Weaving Workshops with Maximo Laura
Study with Peru's Living National Treasure, Maximo Laura, in Arequipa. Renowned tapestry artist and encouraging teacher, Maximo helps you learn his innovative tapestry techniques in three weaving workshops, each three weeks long, for Beginner, Intermediate, and Advanced skill levels.

Personal attention with only five students in each workshop. Maximo is assisted by his nephew Master Weaver Richard Albites.

Easter/Semana Santa Tour to Ayacucho
Tour includes visits to folk and textile artists' studios, artisan markets and villages, hands-on workshops, cultural events, Easter celebration flower carpets, and delicious cuisine. Tour led by Master Weaver Maximo Laura. Maximum 12 participants.

Maximo Laura at his loom.

Classic Workshops Tour: 22 days in Arequipa
Multi-day workshop/classes in hand embroidery, tapestry weaving, braiding, traditional Colca machine embroidery on a treadle sewing machine, drop-spindle spinning, and natural dyeing. Embroidery lessons by Vanesa Canchari and Richard Albites.

www.puchkaperu.com
Contact Sasha McInnes: sasha@puchkaperu.com for information on tours and workshops.

CENTER FOR TRADITIONAL TEXTILES OF CUSCO/Centro de Textiles Tradicionales del Cusco (CTTC)

Tours and Workshops with Nilda Callañaupa Alvarez

My long-time friend Nilda is *the* expert on weaving and spinning of the Cusco area. She organizes dye workshops for my Behind the Scenes groups and will also welcome your requests (in English or Spanish) for visits to meet the weavers at the Away Weaving Association in Chinchero—Nilda's hometown and home to the original group of weavers who started the CTTC. Learn from the masters about the art of weaving in the Andes and browse the CTTC store where you can directly support the weavers through the purchase of their fine textiles. Be sure to call or email ahead so she and the weavers know you are coming and so that an English-speaker is available to guide you. Ask to walk down the street a block from the Away Weaving Association in Chinchero to Nilda's brother's shop of delightful original drawings of cavorting mice and foxes, with beautiful renditions of Chinchero folks in their typical dress. Some of these charming drawings have been made into a children's book, *Beyond the Stones of Machu Picchu: Folk Tales and Stories of Inca Life*, that makes a wonderful souvenir for the little ones.

Nilda can also organize backstrap-loom weaving lessons, natural dye workshops, and longer visits south of Cusco to the village of Pitumarca to meet weavers and knitters. She is a dynamo, dealing with dozens of projects at once, and if she is not available; she will send an able assistant. The CTTC's main office, store, and museum in Cusco can always use volunteers willing to stay at least three months; this is a great way to learn about Andean textiles while helping out this valuable organization.

ADDRESS: 603 Avenida del Sol, Cusco
www.textilescusco.org
nilda.cttc@gmail.com
TEL: +51 084 228117

An extraordinary design by Maximo Laura comes to life as he works in tapestry weave, a pre-Hispanic technique.

FURTHER READING

Callañaupa Alvarez, Nilda. *Weaving in the Peruvian Highlands: Dreaming Patterns, Weaving Memories*. Thrums Books, 2007.

————. *Textile Traditions of Chinchero: A Living Heritage*. Thrums Books, 2012.

————. *Faces of Tradition: Weaving Elders of the Andes*. Thrums Books, 2013.

————. *Secrets of Spinning, Weaving, and Knitting in the Peruvian Highlands*. Thrums Books, 2017.

Dransart, Penelope. *Textiles from the Andes*. Interlink, 2011.

Heckman, Andrea. *Woven Stories: Andean Textiles and Rituals*. University of New Mexico Press, 2003.

LeCount, Cynthia Gravelle. *Andean Folk Knitting: Traditions and Techniques from Peru and Bolivia*. Interweave Press, 1993.

Lewandowski, Marcia. *Andean Folk Knits: Great Designs from Peru, Chile, Argentina, Ecuador, and Bolivia*. Lark Books, 2005.

Miller, Rebecca Stone. *To Weave for the Sun: Ancient Andean Textiles in the Museum of Fine Arts, Boston*. Thames and Hudson, 1994.

Phipps, Elena. *The Peruvian Four-Selvaged Cloth: Ancient Threads*. Fowler Museum, 2013.

Reinhard, Johan. *Discovering the Inca Ice Maiden*. National Geographic, 1998.

Silverman, Gail P. *A Woven Book of Knowledge: Textile Iconography of Cuzco, Peru*. University of Utah Press, 2008.

Van Buskirk, Libby. *Beyond the Stones of Machu Picchu: Folk Tales and Stories of the Andes*. Thrums Books. 2013.

ONLINE

ContemporaryNomad.com: Blog about world-wide travels, including Peru and Bolivia, with great photos and fascinating accounts that will inspire you to get out in the world.

ORGANIZATIONS

Alianza Arkana: A grassroots, intercultural organization committed to the protection, development, and wellbeing of the Peruvian Amazon and the Shipibo-Konibo people. Project "Non Kene" (Shipibo for "Our Designs") responds to requests from indigenous Shipibo women and youth for assistance in their artisanal enterprises. **www.alianzaarkana.org/work/non-kene**

Andean Textile Arts: Supporting the people and communities of the Andes in their efforts to preserve and revitalize their textile traditions. **www.andeantextilearts.org**

ClothRoads: An online marketplace, providing economic support to artisans worldwide. **www.clothroads.com**

Shipibo Joi: A collective of Shipibo women in Yarinacocha who create textiles with unique designs that express their spiritual relationship with the rainforest environment. They also make pottery, seed jewelry and carvings. Their artisan shop called Maroti Shobo has many individual stalls facing the Plaza de Armas in Yarinacocha, just minutes from Pucallpa, at Jr. Aguaytia #443. **www.shipibojoi.wordpress.com**

WARP Weave a Real Peace: A networking organization for textile-based development work. **www.weavearealpeace.org**

PHOTO CREDITS

All photographs are by Cynthia LeCount Samaké except for the following:

Amano Museum: pp. 11, 37

Claudia Avila: p. 58

Center for Traditional Textiles of Cusco: pp. 87, 91

Joe Coca: pp. 6-7, 22, 24-25, 60, 76, 79 (bottom) 80, 81 (bottom), 136

Nacho Calonge / Alamy: p. 132

Edubucher: p. 68

Anthony Eitnier / ContemporaryNomad.com: pp: 3, 88

Diego Grandi / Shutterstock.com: p. 102

Gerardo Guzmán: p. 20

Nigel Hoy: p.61

jjspring / Shutterstock.com: p. 135

Dan Lundberg: p. 119

Kamchatka / Dreamstime.com: pp. 94-95

klublu / Shutterstock.com: p. 101

Larco Museum: p. 38

Sasha McInnes/Puchka Peru Textile Tours: pp. 51, 52, 147

Michell Alpaca: p. 71 (bottom)

Mrallen / Dreamstime.com: p. 98

Byelikova Oksana / Shutterstock.com: p. 131

Pixattitude / Dreamstime.com: p. 79

Leonid Plotkin / Alamy: p. 132

Gustavo Postal / Shutterstock.com: p. 100

Alex Proimos: p. 138

Prosiaczeq / Dreamstime.com: p. 71 (top)

Ksenia Ragozina / Shutterstock.com: p. 9

Jeffrey Roth: p. 78

sharptoyou / Shutterstock.com: p. 53

Cristina Stoian / Dreamstime: p. 81 (top)

John Warburton-Lee / Alamy: p.72

Jack Wheeler / Xapiri.com: p. 35

Wollertz / Dreamstime: p. 66

CAPTIONS

Page 4
Top right: Handknitted chullo from Chinchero, Peru; Lower left: Miniature tapestry weaving from Bolivia.

Page 5: Weaver from Chahuaytire, Peru warping her loom.

Pages 6-7
Left: Tapestry weaver in Potolo, Bolivia. Right: Knitter in the Peruvian Highlands. Bottom: Carnival celebrant in Oruro, Bolivia.

Pages 92–93
Top: Handwoven sash with deer and monster motifs worn at the Anata Andina festival in Oruro, Bolivia; Embellished llama at La Raya Pass market on the road between Cusco and Puno, Peru; Girl in traditional chullo of the Lake Titicaca region, Peru; Girls from Pitumarca, Peru, practicing spinning; Festival musician in beaded chullo from Huacatinco, Peru.

Center: Handknitted chullo with llamas from Bolivia; knitted hat with q'urpus (bobbles) in process from Accha Alta, Peru; Potolo weaver from Bolivia creating a complex tapestry inspired by pre-Hispanic motifs—and her own dreams.

Bottom: Caretaker at Awana Kancha tends the llamas, near Cusco, Peru; Men from Chinchero, Peru, in their festival-fine ponchos and chullos; Women wear their newest and best handwoven awayos for Anata Andina in Oruro, Bolivia; Kiwicha fields.

INDEX

Following page: Dancers in the Fiesta de Virgen del Carmen in Paucartambo, Peru.